# A Guide for Developing an English Curriculum for the Eighties

# A Guide for Developing an English Curriculum for the Eighties

Allan A. Glatthorn
University of Pennsylvania

National Council of Teachers of English
1111 Kenyon Road, Urbana, Illinois 61801

Staff Editor: Barbara Davis

Book Design: Tom Kovacs, interior; Vicki Martin, cover

NCTE Stock Number 19220

Library of Congress Cataloging in Publication Data

Glatthorn, Allan A        1924–

A guide for developing an English curriculum for the eighties.

    Bibliography:    p.
    1. English language—Study and teaching (Secondary)  2. Curriculum planning.        I. Title
LB1631.G56        428.2'07'12        80-26372
ISBN 0-8141-1922-0

# Contents

*Foreword*                                                                    *ix*

*Preface*                                                                    *xiii*

1.  Where Have We Been? A Retrospective Examination            1

2.  Where Are We Now? An Analysis of Present Trends            16

3.  A Process of Incremental Curriculum Development            22

4.  The Mastery Curriculum                                    27

5.  Curriculum Mapping                                        34

6.  Building A Content Planning Matrix                        38

7.  Evaluating and Modifying the
    Content Planning Matrix                                   41

8.  Developing the Syncretic English Curriculum               47

9.  How to Provide for Mandated Competencies:
    Checking on the "Basics"                                  50

10. Using Research Knowledge to Improve
    the Teaching of English                                   54

11. Developing the English Notebook                           69

12. Using Separate Objectives in Integrated Units             74

13. Building English Mastery into
    Interdisciplinary Courses                                 82

14. How to Design Sound Elective Programs                     92

15. Writing Mastery Learning Units                            97

16. A Personal Epilogue: A Curriculum of Meaning            105

| | |
|---|---|
| *Figures* | 110 |
| *Bibliography* | 137 |
| *Author* | 143 |

# List of Figures

1. Relationship of the Five Basic Curriculum Streams    110
2. Planning Calendar for Curriculum Development    111
3. Salient Characteristics of Four Types of Curricula    112
4. Mapping Form for English Language Arts Curriculum Project    113
5. Analysis Form for English Language Arts Curriculum Project    114
6. Evaluating the Content Planning Matrix    115
7. Content Planning Matrix: Composition, Mastery    116
8. Comprehensive Criteria for a Syncretic English Curriculum    117
9. Mastery Objectives Form    120
10. Unit Planning Chart    121
11. Unit Outcomes Chart    122
12. Sample Form for Evaluating High School Humanities Offerings    123
13. Sample Chart Listing Recommendations for Humanities Offerings    125
14. Sample Chart of Themes and Disciplinary Contributions    126
15. Sample Chart of Mastery Content and Unit Placement in English    127
16. Sample Analysis of Weekly Interdisciplinary Unit Emphasis    128
17. Sample Outline of Daily Plans for an Interdisciplinary Unit    129
18. Sample Statement on a Mastery Learning Unit    130
19. Sample Assignment Sheet    131
20. Sample Mastery Grading Form    132
21. Sample Corrective Exercise Form    133

# Foreword

For the past decade the English teaching profession has been in need of some new ideas in curriculum—defined by the National Council of Teachers of English Commission on the English Curriculum as "goals, content, and teaching/learning procedures." A survey of Council publications during the past few years reveals a surprisingly small number of books on curriculum reform. Several explanations can be given for the shortage of useful Council books on curriculum. Among them would certainly be that much professional concentration in recent years has gone into formulating responses to proponents of competency-based teaching, minimal competencies, and state-mandated testing.

Seemingly voiceless against the excesses of an often anti-intellectual movement, teachers have of course turned to their professional organizations for developing positions on these pressing issues and for explaining to the general public the values inherent in teaching and learning which go beyond "minimal standards" and "testable" skills. Indeed, the Commission on the English Curriculum itself devoted two or three years to discussing these issues and advising the Council on ways to counteract the more problematic elements of the CBE (competency-based education) movement. We have tried to be articulate in making our position known and available to the public. Yet, in addressing these issues—which are perhaps as much political as educational—we have had limited time and inclination to concern ourselves with our central charge— to contribute substantive research and new ideas in the area of curriculum.

While it is clear that we have a professional responsibility to protest against legislation that strikes us as educationally counterproductive, we also have a responsibility to continue to do research in our field and to publish our findings for the general instruction of teachers at all levels. Against a background of continued resistance to misguided legislative mandates, we have to persist in saying that on the basis of our ongoing research and in-class professional experience, we have something to contribute toward directing the future of teaching and learning in the language arts. With this new book, one such positive statement asserts itself clearly.

A real need in recent years has been for the publication of practical books with good advice for teachers and administrators who, restrained and controlled by state and local requirements, must face the challenge of creating workable curricula in English—curricula that reflect teachers' knowledge of their field, students' learning needs, school administrators' requirements, state pressures, and parental concern. At the same time, there is a need for books that reflect an awareness of the available research in content areas, pedagogy, and curriculum study. Finally, there is a need for more responsible journalism about why Johnny and Mary can't read and write and more solid advice from true, dedicated professionals— that is, trained students of the language arts who know intimately the challenging responsibilities of teacher, administrator, scholar, parent—and who can focus on the problems in constructive ways. Without slipping into faddism or doomsday talk, Allan Glatthorn has fulfilled many of these felt needs.

In *A Guide for Developing an English Curriculum for the Eighties*, Professor Glatthorn, past Director of the NCTE Commission on the English Curriculum, argues for a curriculum in language arts which is true to the intellectual and emotional needs of students while being accountable to society's expectations for a curriculum which is practical and oriented toward skills. Glatthorn's message is that curriculum must do more than merely provide students with survival skills. It must be challenging and coherent. The school owes it to the student and taxpayer alike to provide a curriculum which is rich in content, capable of increasing student skills, testable in areas where testing matters and can be successfully achieved, responsive to and supportive of areas of language acquisition that are not testable, and cognizant of learners' needs and abilities. For Glatthorn, this curriculum—well within the reach of any school willing to commit itself to quality education—must be genuinely accountable to the parent and the legislature. Glatthorn makes it clear that parents and the public at large should have a say in the creation of goals, content, and methods in the classroom, but he argues persuasively for the preeminent role of professional educators in designing and developing curriculum. He is respectful toward the various state mandates for testing minimal competencies (who among us does not want high school graduates to be able to read tax forms and road maps?) but he raises two important issues: What are the *real* basic competencies necessary for life as it will be lived during the remainder of the century? What price does the student (and society) pay for an educational system that equates basic competencies with life-survival skills at the lowest affective and intellectual levels and at the expense of all enrichment programs?

Never ignoring or maligning the realities of the CBE movement of the seventies, Glatthorn suggests strategies for developing mature curricula that will use the strengths of CBE while transcending its weaknesses. He is wise enough to know that a guide for the perplexed must acknowledge and confront the present perplexities in a realistic and even a gracious spirit.

Professor Glatthorn argues for a so-called mastery curriculum, but he restricts the approach to areas in which mastery is known to be an effective method. Not a proselytizer, he suggests that the identification of mastery components needs to be accomplished early in the process of creating a viable curriculum. He legislates nothing; to the contrary, he calls for the fullest participation of teachers, planners, and parents in exploring what can be mastered in the study of English. Arguing against some of the approaches of the past (he traces five, beginning with the progressive functionalism of 1917–1940 and ending with the current emphasis on privatistic conservatism) as well as against various curricular extravagances, he suggests that the mastery curriculum is the most cost-efficient and yet intellectually effective system because it views English "through several perspectives" while focusing curriculum development "on only a certain portion of that curriculum."

For Glatthorn the mastery curriculum should be characterized by what he calls "syncretic orientation"—that is, it should draw from what we know to be our rich content resources, our knowledge of cognitive development in children, the students' own sense of personal relevance, and expectations of society. But even though mastery is enhanced by contributions from all these sources, the actual curriculum is comprised of only those aspects of learning which participating teachers, planners, students, and parents agree are "essential" and capable of "careful structuring." I hasten to add that Glatthorn never rules out or diminishes the importance of aspects of the study of English that do not lend themselves to "careful structuring"—such as the so-called organic curriculum which focuses on affective response. He points out that it is "extravagant" to spend time planning an area of curriculum that does not lend itself to structuring. ("The organic curriculum is just as essential as the mastery curriculum but it is different in one crucial way: it is nonstructured. . . . It is best facilitated not by graded, structured units of study but by a sensitive teacher responding to the emergent needs of the learner.")

*A Guide for Developing an English Curriculum for the Eighties*
is not bedside reading—though it is written in lucid, well-organized
prose. It is, in fact, a practical *guide:* a step-by-step plan for developing an English curriculum to be used in the hard light of day.
While very tightly structured, reflecting Glatthorn's careful analysis
of a complex situation as well as his years of personal experience
with what does and does not work, the book's plan can be modified
in a dozen different ways to fit the requirements of real teachers
in real schools. Glatthorn specifically suggests some modifications.
The author is modest in suggesting that his plan need not be followed scrupulously; I would say that the book warrants close
attention to its detailed suggestions before the reader moves off in
a different direction. Glatthorn has probably thought through the
alternatives already and suggested the one(s) most likely to produce
results. In context, some of his ideas may sound somewhat complex;
in actual practice, the usefulness of his approach would surely
disclose itself.

Professor Glatthorn is interested in providing the student with a
powerful, sensible language arts experience. The student who goes
through Glatthorn's curriculum can be expected to meet the
minimal-competency requirements of any state education department while mastering what teachers feel to be the basics—or rather
the essentials—of solid academic experiences in reading, writing,
speaking, and listening. Glatthorn's curriculum plan also allows the
teacher the fullest freedom in designing courses and exploring
personal teaching styles. His instincts are nothing if not generous;
he advises, he does not dictate. It will surely be in the best interest
of all of us—teachers and curriculum planners—to learn from this
experienced colleague as we face the perplexities of the years ahead.

> Barrett J. Mandel
> Director, NCTE Commission on
> the English Curriculum (1978-
> 1980)

# Preface

I write out of a sense of both frustration and hope. The frustration derives from my experience in working with coordinators, department heads, and curriculum committees to produce English language arts curriculum guides—which, too often, turned out to be excellent documents that very soon were filed and forgotten. The hope derives from a sincere belief in the ability of both curriculum workers and teachers to find a better way of translating their knowledge and experience into more usable curriculum materials.

The monograph is addressed to the instructional leader of English. I use the term "instructional leader" to include all who have direct responsibility for providing leadership in the area of English curriculum. The audience, therefore, includes principals, assistant principals, district coordinators, department heads, team leaders, curriculum committees, and classroom teachers with special assignments—anyone responsible for improving the English program.

My chief concern is with the secondary English curriculum, although from time to time I refer to the elementary program in areas where continuity is important. The purpose of this monograph is to explain a process for improving the English curriculum. My hope is that the process will work in any school district and can be used by anyone without special training in curriculum development. I do not propose some ideal English curriculum, because I do not believe that there is one best curriculum. And I have tried to make the explanations as simple as possible because I want this to be a do-it-yourself manual that requires no special training or outside help.

I am indebted to several colleagues and friends who have provided continuing help in this endeavor. Allan Dittmer, Barrett Mandel, and Beverly Busching, leaders of important NCTE committees and commissions, encouraged me and generously shared materials. Herbert Adams, my colleague and friend at Science Research Associates, reassured me of the long-term value of what I was doing. Pauline Degenfelder, Dolores Drewniak, Pat Eyring, Mildred Dougherty, and Hugh Cassell, friends and colleagues in districts where these ideas were first tested, gave me the benefit of their experience and insight. Paul O'Dea of NCTE provided the kind of editorial guidance that all authors need. Ruth Ebert, secretary par excellence, helped immeasurably by proofreading, raising questions, and typing. And my wife, Barbara P. Glatthorn, was of more help than she will ever know.

I close with one special acknowledgment of intellectual indebtedness. Much of the content of Chapter 1 is based upon Arthur N. Applebee's *Tradition and Reform in the Teaching of English.* I consider his book the basic text in the history of our field, and I strongly recommend it to any reader interested in a more detailed history of our profession.

# 1 Where Have We Been?
# A Retrospective Examination

Before beginning with some proposals concerning a process of curriculum development, it would be well to examine where we have been and where we are now in the teaching of English. The retrospective examination undertaken in this chapter will be useful because it should provide a needed perspective about both the present and the future. And a careful analysis of what is happening now, which will be undertaken in Chapter 2, should provide additional data in determining which curriculum processes are likely to be most effective.

A look back at the currents in the English curriculum over the past sixty years suggests that there have been five distinct periods in that history. There is, of course, an arbitrariness always in delineating so-called periods of history demarcated by specific dates, for history more often seems like a running stream that cannot be so channelled. With that warning in mind, however, we probably can make more sense out of our past if we make some divisions, attempt to define the essential nature of each period, and identify some major developments. This framework is therefore suggested as a way of looking at the recent history of the English curriculum:

| Dates | Period |
|-------|--------|
| 1917–1940 | Progressive functionalism |
| 1941–1956 | Developmental conformism |
| 1957–1967 | Scholarly structuralism |
| 1968–1974 | Romantic radicalism |
| 1975– | Privatistic conservatism |

## Progressive Functionalism

The first period, here called progressive functionalism, was that time between the two wars, embracing the high spirits of the 1920s, the crash of 1929–1932, and the struggle toward recovery in the

1

thirties. There was a new interest in science and technology, brought into focus by the 1939 World's Fair; there was much talk about scientific management and the need for efficiency; and there was a belief that the nation's problems could be solved by legislation. In brief, it was the age of Hoover the engineer and Roosevelt the reformer.

In psychology, two strong forces were at work. E. L. Thorndike was promulgating the need for the scientific measurement of intelligence and achievement, and Kurt Lewin and other Gestalt psychologists were insisting on the importance of the unified experience. Similarly, in curriculum, two divergent theories seemed influential. William Kilpatrick (1918), a disciple of John Dewey, argued for an experience-centered curriculum oriented toward social reform. On the other hand, Franklin Bobbitt (1924) was convinced that the curriculum should be built scientifically, by first analyzing the life needs of the learner, then specifying objectives derived from those needs.

The English curriculum developments of the period reflected both the mood of the nation and the theories of the experts. It can be called a period of progressive functionalism because it seemed to be characterized by progressive rhetoric and functional intent. The first major NCTE curriculum publication, *An Experience Curriculum in English* (Hatfield, 1935), clearly reflects an attempt to synthesize both of these elements. The rhetoric was clearly progressive: "Experience is the best of all schools . . . The ideal curriculum consists of well-selected experiences." The basic element of instruction should be the "radical progressive unit," organized into "experience strands," "arranged like broad easy stair steps in a reasonably steady progression of intellectual difficulty and social maturity" (p. viii). But the content was unabashedly functional, strongly influenced by Bobbitt's theories of curriculum. For example, the first strand, "social conversation," emphasized such utilitarian activities as making small talk with acquaintances, holding a conversation with friends' parents, and congratulating a friend. Other units were concerned with so-called life competencies (to borrow a current term to describe an older approach) such as making a telephone call, holding an interview, and conducting a discussion.

The period of progressive functionalism was also marked by certain interesting pedagogical innovations, two of which took different approaches toward individualizing instruction. The Dalton or contract plan (Dewey, 1922) required individual students to make a contract with the teacher, covering the amount of work to be learned within a given period and the grade toward which the student aspired. Much of the time, of course, the student worked independently, although some teachers added group discussions of reading in response to criticism that the plan stressed too much isolation in the learning process. The other approach, the so-called mastery units advocated by Morrison (1926), divided the curriculum into a series of functional units; each student worked through a unit at a self-paced rate, proceeding to the next only when mastery had been demonstrated. And the NCTE's Committee on Correlation (Weeks, 1936) reported beginning attempts to correlate the study of English with other disciplines.

Two separate studies conducted by Dora Smith in the 1930s suggested that the classroom teacher was, perhaps predictably, somewhat eclectic in approach. The first study, *Instruction in English* (1933), based upon an analysis of 156 courses of study, was somewhat optimistic in its conclusions. The unit method of instruction seemed to have taken hold. There was evidence of attempts to individualize, either through ability grouping or contracts, and there was less uniformity than there had been previously in the selection of literature; she noted with some optimism that there was "evidence in classroom practice that some teachers are able to follow a course of study organized by types without undue stress on form and technique" (pp. 47–49). The second study (Smith, 1941), based more upon direct observation of actual practice, was less encouraging. In her analysis of English instruction in fifty-one school systems in New York, she found less evidence of progressive reform. The single text seemed to determine the curriculum. The classroom was teacher-dominated: "Question and answer procedures with the teacher in command, and recitation around the room of sentences written out at home the night before represented by far the most common activities of the average high school English class in New York" (p. 253). And attempts to individualize were restricted largely to administrative arrangements. The classroom teacher taught the whole class: "regimentation was the rule; individualization the exception" (p. 157).

## Developmental Conformism

The second period in the history of the English curriculum, developmental conformism, essentially spanned the years of the Truman and Eisenhower presidencies. Except, of course, for the war years, that period in retrospect seems to have been an era of national tranquility. The postwar recession predicted by the experts never materialized; in fact, there was a remarkable postwar boom. Fears of communism and anxiety about McCarthyism made people uneasy, and the Supreme Court desegregation decision of 1954 suggested that there were deeper problems that should be confronted; but the national mood seemed to be one of optimism. The nation seemed strong, and its problems appeared to be manageable.

In the field of psychology, Havighurst's *Developmental Tasks and Education* (1948) seemed most important. In this work, which had an immediate and direct influence on curriculum development in English and other fields, Havighurst outlined the major stages in life, from preschool to the graduate level. For each stage he identified important characteristics and needs, suggesting the kinds of learning outcomes and activities that would be most appropriate. The most influential curriculum theorists were probably Ralph Tyler and Hilda Taba. Tyler's *Basic Principles of Curriculum and Instruction* (1950), which began as a syllabus for his graduate course at the University of Chicago, reduced decisions about curriculum planning to four basic questions: What educational purposes should the school seek to attain? What educational experiences can be provided that are likely to attain these purposes? How can these educational experiences be effectively organized? How can we determine whether these purposes are being attained?

What has come to be known as the Tyler rationale continues to be the basic paradigm for most curriculum workers today. Taba, strongly influenced by Gestalt psychologists, antedated the Brunerians in insisting, in contradistinction to Bobbitt, that the curriculum should be concerned with the larger organizing ideas, which were more powerful because they subsumed many smaller discrete elements. Her work in developing materials for intergroup education, however, had a more immediate impact than her curriculum theories. Applebee's assessment of her contribution in *Tradition and Reform in the Teaching of English* (1974, p. 149) seems to be a fair one:

> The work of these [intergroup relations] institutes, of the project staff, and of the cooperating sschools led to a long series of publications on human relations and intergroup education; these presented teachers throughout the country with practical, school-based approaches for all age levels and in many different curriculum areas. Nevertheless there were major difficulties in the approach

Taba and her staff advocated. The fundamental problem was
naiveté . . . which saw racial problems in the limited context of
attitudes and dispositions rather than as manifestations of deeper
institutional and economic forces.

While Tyler's ideas about design and Taba's concerns with intergroup relations were clearly influencing many professional leaders,
the most significant curriculum movement of the period developed
from the efforts of educational bureaucrats, not the theories of
scholars. Life adjustment education, which, as a slogan at least, was
the most important development of the 1950s, was sired by the
National Education Association (NEA) and the U.S. Office of
Education. The Educational Policies Commission of the NEA in its
first report, *Education for All American Youth* (1944), recommended for all schools a core program of so-called common learnings which would help young people learn such skills as getting
along with others, becoming a useful family member, and choosing
a useful vocation. The U.S. Office of Education followed by establishing a Commission on Life Adjustment Education for Youth,
which attempted to set up a series of "action programs" across the
nation to achieve the goals of life adjustment. Even though the
proponents of life adjustment education attempted to minimize
the conformist nature of the movement when critics began to attack,
their underlying message seemed clear: This was a good society,
and the goal of education was to learn to adjust to it.

Life adjustment education seemed to enjoy a mixed reception
in the English profession. While there were many leaders in the
profession who attacked its basic tenets, it seemed to have a subtle
but pervasive influence. The major curriculum project undertaken
by the NCTE Commission on the English Curriculum, which cul-
minated in a five-volume report, seemed to reflect the influence
of both Havighurst and the life adjustment "educationists," as
they were coming to be known. Hence it has been labeled a period
of developmental conformism. As noted in the third volume of
the Commission's report, *The English Language Arts in the Secondary School* (1956), the English curriculum was to take cognizance
of the inner pressures resulting from the development of the learner
—but was also to respond to the external pressures of the society.
And the specific nature of that response was to be the product of
a consensus of the various interest groups of the community to
be served.

The interest in correlating English with other subjects, which
began in the previous period, developed into perhaps the major

pedagogical innovation of the forties and fifties—the core curriculum. As implemented in most of the experimental schools, the core curriculum was an attempt to integrate learnings from several disciplines by having students study broad themes related both to adolescent interests and societal trends. The core curriculum was widely touted by professors of curriculum who saw it as a way out of "sterile traditionalism," but it never really appealed to most classroom teachers. Applebee (1974) notes that a study conducted by Grace S. Wright (1950) for the U.S. Office of Education found that only 3.5 percent of junior and senior high course offerings showed any attempt to correlate content from two or more disciplines.

However, there was evidence in the classroom that teachers were attempting to integrate language arts, at least. Arno Jewett's (1959) survey of 285 courses of study conducted at the end of this period found that the predominant pattern of curriculum organization was a thematic or topical unit which integrated several phases of English; and the junior high courses showed a genuine attempt to develop those units around the interests and needs of younger adolescents. He also noted that many of the curriculum guides included units on relevant topics such as critical thinking, propaganda analysis, semantics, and the nature of communication. While Jewett admitted that the courses of study he examined probably reflected a more innovative spirit than those not studied, his findings relative to the widespread use of thematic units are supported, partially at least, by James Olson's (1969) study of literature anthologies commonly used in the school. In comparing the anthologies used in 1957 and in 1946, Olson found the later books to be more concerned with thematic units and greater representation of literary selections relating to the concerns of the young.

## Scholarly Structuralism

The third period of curriculum history, the era of academic rationalism, was the decade 1957–1967, which embraced the Kennedy and Johnson presidencies. In a sense it was the beginning of two decades of national trauma. Both the successful launching of Sputnik and the assassination of John Kennedy seriously battered the nation's confidence, as evidenced by the severe questioning of the quality of our schools. But those schools were expanding rapidly. During this period, student enrollments increased by 33 percent and the number of teachers by 50 percent. It was also a period of legislative activism, with the passage of some twenty-four pieces of major educational legislation.

This was a time when scholars from the academy were most influential in the schools. School people turned to the studies of Jean Piaget to learn how children developed, to the works of B. F. Skinner to discover how children could be controlled, and to the theories of Jerome Bruner to discover how children could be taught. It is interesting to note in the case of both Piaget and Bruner that these two psychologists also had the greatest impact on the school curriculum. In curriculum circles it was *de rigueur* to cite Piaget's developmental theories and Bruner's strictures on structure.

Hence I see it as a time of scholarly structuralism, when curriculum leaders believed that the theories and research of academicians, rationally applied, could be used to develop "teacher-proof" curricula, based upon the structure of the discipline.

Urged on by NCTE's *The National Interest and the Teaching of English* (1961), the federal government took a more active interest in the field of English. The U.S. Office of Education Cooperative Research Program was expanded in 1961 to include English, providing funds for what came to be known as Project English; and the National Defense Education Act of 1964 provided funds for the teaching of English and reading. These federal funds provided needed support for research, curriculum centers, and numerous summer institutes.

Perhaps the most important professional publication of the period was *Freedom and Discipline in English* (1965), a report of the College Entrance Examination Board's Commission on English, which again recommended a consensus curriculum, but one built upon the so-called tripod of language, literature, and composition. This recommendation was reflected in much of the curriculum work developed under the aegis of Project English, but Arthur Applebee (1974, p. 197) notes that "the commission's greatest success, however, came not from its recommendations in *Freedom and Discipline*, but from a series of summer institutes during the summer of 1962."

However, neither the publication nor the institutes seemed to have much effect on the classroom teacher, according to the results of a major study conducted by James R. Squire and Roger K. Applebee (1968). In 158 schools, which seemed to have excellent English programs, Squire and Applebee discovered that more than half of class time was spent in the teaching of literature with little attempt to integrate the English language arts. Use of the lecture and recitation predominated; small group activities and audiovisual aids were infrequently employed. While reporting evidence of much sound teaching in college preparatory programs, the authors also noted glaring weaknesses in programs for terminal students.

This period was also a time of extensive pedagogical innovation. Simply reciting the many labels suggests the extent of the desire to try something new: team teaching, modular scheduling, independent study, individualized instruction, large group instruction, small group instruction, middle schools, house plans. And, largely under the impetus of Charles Keller and his John Jay Hay Fellows program, English teachers led in developing new "humanities" programs, which often turned out to be intellectualized core programs under another name. The period was also characterized by new interest in gifted students, as department heads anxiously developed accelerated courses based upon the most recent advanced placement examinations. And, primarily in reaction to the protest by black activists, belated attention was given to black language and literature.

### Romantic Radicalism

The term *romantic radicalism* is used to describe the fourth period, 1968–1974, because so much of the rhetoric of the time seemed to couple a romantic Rousseauan view of the child with a radical critique of the schools and the society. It was the era of the Apollo moon landing, Civil Rights protests, the assassinations of Robert Kennedy and Martin Luther King, Vietnam, and Watergate—a time when the nation seemed to reel from the series of traumatic shocks.

At such a time people began turning inward, worrying about their deeper feelings and "true selves." Sensitivity groups flourished, and the psychological theories of Carl Rogers became almost dogma. In his chief work on education, *Freedom to Learn* (1969), Rogers disparaged the act of teaching, insisting that the only real growth emerged from within the self and another person could only facilitate such self-directed learning—a view also advocated by many exponents of open education. It is significant, perhaps, that no one curriculum writer can be singled out as the chief theorist of open education. In fact, one might infer from the writings of those advocating the open classroom that the curriculum was really unimportant. If one created an open classroom environment, appropriately provisioned, the curriculum would emerge organically from the inquiries of the learners.

In the field of English the most important occurrence during this fourth period was probably the Dartmouth Conference. Held in the summer of 1966, the conference brought together approximately fifty specialists in the teaching of English from England and the United States. In the view of many observers, the main contribution of the conference was that it enabled the British teachers and scholars to educate their American counterparts. As reported in two companion volumes (Muller, 1967; Dixon, 1967), the British educators persuaded almost all the American participants that the British had the answers: child-centered curriculum, concern for the language of the child, use of improvisational drama, the primacy of informal discussion as the instructional mode, and the encouragement of imaginative writing—all were seen as infinitely superior to an American curriculum still concerned for the structure of the discipline.

Both open education and the child-centered English curriculum, were British imports. Yet, perhaps not surprisingly, it was a home-grown American idea—the elective system—which had the greatest impact on classrooms in this country. While Applebee (1974) dates the first electives as being offered in the University of Iowa laboratory school in 1960 and George Hillocks (1972) cites a 1955 *English Journal* article as the first published description of an elective program, the grassroots movement really seemed to catch hold in the late sixties. After surveying "over one hundred [elective] programs," Hillocks (1972, p. 123) concluded his "critical appraisal" with this optimistic assessment:

> Given the time to study, plan, and evaluate their work, English teachers, with their newly awakened sense of professional dignity and responsibility, may manage to revolutionize the teaching of English for all students, where the best efforts of the special centers have failed. For that result alone, elective programs, whether they be passing fancies or the beginning of a new tradition, will have been worth the effort.

Not everyone, of course, shared Hillocks's enthusiasm. Paul Copperman (1978, pp. 96–97) was among many who held the elective system partly responsible for the decline in SAT scores:

> The weakness in the current elective system is that it enables a student to avoid the kind of rigorous work he needs to develop his primary academic skills. . . . As interesting as many of the above-listed electives appear, most of them do not provide the type of disciplined training that students need in order to develop their skills.

## Privatistic Conservatism

The present period of our history, called privatistic conservatism, seems essentially conservative in educational philosophy; yet the conservatism is motivated by a narcissistic obsession with the private self. Since there is so little historical perspective it is difficult to date the period precisely. Some might use 1971 as the beginning, when the Michigan Accountability Act was passed; others would argue for the passage of the Oregon competency law in 1972. My own sense is that 1974—the year of the *Lau* v. *Nichols* decision mandating bilingual education—might be a more appropriate dividing line. While we might disagree with the precise beginning of the period, we can readily agree about the national mood. It is a time of inflation and gas lines, taxpayers' rebellions, worry about declining test scores, and increased fault-finding with the schools. And it is a period marked by what in the long-run may be even more significant: the "peaceful Latino invasion," which raised the Latino population to twenty million.

From an educator's point of view, the most influential psychologist is probably Benjamin Bloom, whose major work, *Human Characteristics and School Learning* (1976), provides the theory and research for the concept of mastery learning. In the curriculum field, W. James Popham and John Goodlad would probably be singled out as most influential. Popham seems to represent the best curricular technologists who have made the Tyler rationale more respectable with additional refinements and technical labels. And Goodlad, as noted in the next chapter, has given us a new way of looking at the entire field.

As yet there is no major professional publication which either encapsulates present trends or suggests a new direction. There is, however, much talk at the leadership level of the Bullock report from England, *A Language for Life* (1975), which according to Brunetti (1978, p. 64) ". . . provides some thoughtful ideas on how English language programs should be organized and conducted and some excellent suggestions in the directions our English teaching profession should move in over the next few years." There is also a 1980 publication of the National Council of Teachers of English Commission on the Curriculum titled *Three Language-Arts Curriculum Models: Pre-Kindergarten through College.* The articles in this book, written by experienced teachers and curriculum planners, outline the competencies, process, and heritage approaches to curriculum planning as applied to all levels of instruction.

In such a time when *innovative* seems to be a pejorative, one would not expect to find—and indeed does not find—much pedagogical experimentation. Aside from widespread interest in mastery learning, some evidence of a recurring concern for the gifted, and much talk about the basics of English, the period seems to be one in which classroom teachers are sitting back and waiting.

This picture of English teachers of the late seventies, cautiously refining older practices, is substantiated by a recent survey of 316 secondary schools conducted by Arthur Applebee (1978). He notes the following trends: the widespread adoption of elective programs (at the twelfth grade level, in 78 percent of the schools); classes for the gifted (in 45 percent); remedial classes (in 71 percent); small group work (in 75 percent); and competency examinations (in 43 percent).

## A Review of Sixty Years of Educational Development

In reflecting on that past, let us focus on four important trends that are relevant to our concern for curriculum planning: the pace of change, the general orientation of the curriculum, the nature of pedagogical innovations, and the practice of the classroom teacher.

Regarding the pace of change, one can readily observe that the length of each period of educational development has grown shorter. The first period, as noted above, lasted for twenty-three years; the next, fifteen; the third, ten; and the fourth, six years. It would be foolhardy, of course, to make too much of this. It well may be that more recent periods seem shorter only because they are closer to us. Yet the data do give credence to the conventional wisdom that change is occurring more rapidly.

In reflecting upon the general orientation of the curriculum during these past six decades, I spent some time searching for an appropriate metaphor. When most educators speak about the general directions of the curriculum past and present, they seize initially on the analogy of the pendulum, which suggests short swings between extreme positions. Or they talk of cycles, a more abstract figure which suggests longer periods of recurring tendencies. Neither metaphor seems to portray the past sixty years of English. Instead, we might think of separate streams that continue to flow—at times swollen, at times almost dry; at times separate, at times joining. In identifying such streams in our curricular history, some useful terms are those proposed by Elliott W. Eisner (1979) for his "five basic orientations in the curriculum." Those orientations, as he defines them, are:

1. *Development of Cognitive Processes* (p. 51): ". . . the major functions of the school are (1) to help children learn how to learn and (2) to provide them with the opportunities to use and strengthen the variety of intellectual faculties that they possess."

2. *Academic Rationalism* (p. 54): ". . . the major function of the school is to foster the intellectual growth of the student in those subject matters most worthy of study."

3. *Personal Relevance* (p. 57): ". . . emphasizes the primacy of personal meaning. . . . The curriculum is to emerge out of the sympathetic interaction of teachers and students. . . ."

4. *Social Adaptation and Social Reconstruction* (p. 62): ". . . derives its aims and content from an analysis of the society the school is designed to serve."

5. *Curriculum as Technology* (p. 67): ". . . conceives of curriculum planning as being essentially a technical undertaking. . . . The central problem of the technological orientation to curriculum is not to question ends but rather to operationalize them through statements that are referenced to observable behavior."

These five curricular orientations are seen as streams that have always been present throughout our recent history. Figure 1 suggests schematically how these streams have ebbed and flowed throughout the five periods of our history. It shows how their strength has varied and how, during a given period, one or two have predominated. And, to a great extent, it shows that the strength of a given orientation at a particular period of time seems to have resulted from powerful social forces impinging upon the schools.

In turning to the third issue in curriculum planning mentioned above—that of pedagogical innovations—one is first inclined toward the cynical reaction that we keep reinventing the wheel. At first blush such cynicism seems warranted if we consider these so-called innovations of the seventies and their historical antecedents:

| *Innovation* | *Historical Antecedent* |
|---|---|
| Competency-based education | Franklin Bobbitt's theories, 1924 |
| Mastery learning | Henry Morrison's mastery units, 1926 |

| | |
|---|---|
| Humanities courses | Core programs, 1930s |
| Individualized learning | Dalton plan, 1922 |

But such a superficial reaction can be misleading. Let me suggest why I believe it is misleading by staying with the metaphor of a wheel. The wheel was a sound idea—one that will always be with us. It can be reinvented profitably, with refinements made possible by a new technology. And the reinvention process is always exciting for the inventor. So the ideas behind these innovations are essentially sound; they have been improved each time they were reintroduced. And the process of developing and implementing innovation was a healthful one for the schools. The only caution, of course, is that we should not be misled by enthusiastic reinventors who claim they have made the perfect wheel.

## Reaction to Change

Such an attitude of cautious openness to change is one that should be recommended to all English teachers. Have they in fact manifested such an attitude? We have the answer, I believe, in the studies of actual classroom practice which, fortunately, have been conducted throughout these six decades. First, observe that English teachers have largely ignored the exhortation to make radical changes in the way in which they teach. Such resistance has discomfited reformers who, like the author, fulminated against such traditional practices as teacher selection of content, the use of factual questions, and reliance upon teacher-led groups. The irony, of course, is that there is now a body of research which suggests that such traditional teaching is most likely to bring about significant gains in achievement. Barak Rosenshine (1979, p. 52) concludes a recent review of research on teaching with this summary:

> The research to date also suggests that the following instructional variables are usually associated with content covered, academically engaged minutes, and achievement gain: teachers maintaining a strong academic focus with encouragement and concern for the academic progress of each student; teacher, rather than student, selection of activities; grouping of students into small and large groups for instruction; and using factual questions and controlled practice in teacher-led groups. In addition the frequency of nonacademic activities such as arts and crafts, reading stories to a group, or questions to students about their personal experience usually are negatively related to achievement gains. This overall pattern might be labeled "direct instruction."

Observe also, however, that there has been a slow but steady change in the teaching of English. Teachers in elective courses are using paperbacks as the basis of small group discussions of literature. That scene is not the ideal envisioned by James Moffett, John Holt, or Neil Postman, but neither is it as bleak a picture as they and other critics allege.

Note, finally, that these teachers have been prudently eclectic in their orientation to the curriculum. Rather than committing themselves completely to a single orientation, they have, as far as can be determined, absorbed into their practice something of each orientation. They cling to the discipline, but without the fervor of the academic rationalists. They teach the cognitive processes, but not to the exclusion of all else. They consciously or unconsciously shape the curriculum in terms of shifting societal trends. They use bits and pieces of a technological approach where that seems appropriate. And, out of choice or necessity, they respond as best as they can to the needs of the students before them.

If the past is indeed prologue, then the following developments seem likely for the immediate future and will of necessity impinge upon the process for developing the curriculum, the content of the curriculum, and the format in which the curriculum is delivered:

1. We probably face several shorter periods of change. The present period of privatistic conservatism will probably run its course within a year or two. We need to find a "quick fix" process for improving the curriculum.

2. The content of the English curriculum will continue to be influenced by all the orientations identified by Eisner (1979), and teachers will continue to be eclectic in their own orientation. Any major curriculum project which commits itself exclusively to a single orientation in the selection of content will probably not be accepted by the classroom teacher.

3. There will continue to be refinements and improvements in the way we group for instruction, in the way we utilize staff, in the way we teach, and in the bases upon which we organize the curriculum. (Some of these refinements will give us a sense of *déjà vu*; note, for example, that the *English Journal* for February 1980 was devoted to the theme of "interdisciplinary English.") And there will be some radical changes, as will be noted in the next chapter, brought about by new technological developments. Also, English teachers will probably ignore exhortations to make radical changes in

their teaching styles. These conclusions suggest that the format of the curriculum needs to be flexible, able to accommodate a variety of teaching methods and organizational styles, without requiring a radical change in the way teachers teach.

But it would be folly, of course, simply to read the future in terms of the past. These are different times, and there are some major developments occurring in the society and in the schools that are likely to have a strong influence on the English curriculum. It is to this matter that the next chapter addresses itself.

# 2 Where Are We Now?
## An Analysis of Present Trends

In what ways is the present different from the past? What developments now are likely to affect our decisions about the curriculum? Examining these questions is more fruitful than fanciful speculation about the distant future. My preference is to let the distant future take care of itself and to plan instead for the short-term future by both learning from the past, as was attempted in Chapter 1, and by extrapolating from present evidence. Seven developments occurring now are worthy of serious attention.

### Analyzing the Art of Teaching

The first development is the increasing power of a stable teaching profession. Applebee's survey (1978, p. 48) indicated that "the typical English department studied had only one new staff member at the beginning of the academic year; only about a third of these new staff members were new to teaching." And those experienced teachers will continue to insist more strongly on explicit authority over matters of the curriculum.

Ole Sand (1971, pp. 223-224), director of the Center for the Study of Instruction for the National Education Association, sounded this note nearly a decade ago:

> . . . the potential of the organized teaching profession to improve the curriculum remains unexploited. One possibility for negotiation in curriculum is the formation and utilization of active and responsive instructional improvement centers at the level of the local association—at the level of the teacher himself.

The implication here is obvious: Future curriculum planning must provide for significant contributions from the instructional staff.

The second factor is the shortage of discretionary funds in school district budgets. Taxpayers continue to resist additional school taxes when enrollments are declining. Inflation necessitates substantial increases in district budgets for maintenance and operating expenses. Teachers' salaries continue to rise, absorbing an increasingly greater part of the total budget. And superintendents and boards react in predictable fashion: They reduce the size of the supervisory staff and sharply limit the funds available for curriculum development. The days of large-scale local curriculum projects are over; the funds are just not available.

The third factor is continuing technological change. Several signs suggest that personal computers and videocassette and disc machines will be commonplace in both homes and schools some five years hence, and new information systems will change both our understanding of the educational process and the way in which students learn. Consider, for example, the implications of a new information service reported in *Time* (9 July 1979). Called "The Source," the service will give users of home computers access to a pool of information derived from more than two thousand separate computer programs, ranging from wine guides to horoscopes.

The fourth major factor is the importance of the state's role in curriculum development. In the past, the state has played chiefly an advisory role in determining the school's curriculum. From time to time, of course, state legislators have turned to curriculum solutions for social problems—mandating courses in Americanism, alcohol and drug education, or driver training, for example. But prior to 1975 they had never interposed themselves in determining local curricula. Now that seems to have changed. As of October 1978, thirty-six states had taken some type of action in support of competency-based education (Pipho, 1978). And 37 percent of the schools surveyed by Applebee (1978) reported that they were using statewide competency tests. While many of these states give local districts some latitude in determining competencies, there are strong pressures in every state to place more emphasis on the basic skills of reading and writing. Although I personally am opposed to much of what competency-based education seems to stand for, I am convinced that any successful curriculum planning for the eighties needs to take realistic cognizance of state mandates.

The fifth factor is our increasing body of knowledge about the processes of teaching and learning. While teaching will always be more art than science, and while the unique interaction of teacher and student will always elude precise scientific analysis, there is a growing volume of research about student achievement and teacher effectiveness. Some of the findings are contradictory, but we begin to see important patterns. After reviewing 289 empirical studies of teacher effectiveness, Donald M. Medley (1979, p. 16) made this observation:

> Despite its shortcomings . . . process-product research can produce, and has produced, reliable information about the nature of effective teaching. When teachers are visited by observers trained to record their behavior accurately and objectively, appropriate analysis of records reveals stable differences between behaviors of teachers who are more effective and those who are less effective in helping pupils grow in basic skills as well as in some affective areas.

In the past, when curriculum theorists admonished practitioners to check the research, the practitioners often justifiably responded by denigrating that research. Now there is no longer any excuse. A curriculum for the eighties must reflect not our biases and our conventional wisdom—but the best available knowledge we have about our subject, the act of teaching, and the process of learning.

The sixth factor is the continuing dissatisfaction with the schools as expressed by parents and the general public. It is unlikely that the schools will show dramatic improvement, given the shortage of funds, the power of a stable teaching profession, and the increasing magnitude of the task of educating indifferent youth. And schools will continue to be a convenient scapegoat for the frustration and anger people feel about the society itself. So we must continue to be responsive to the public we serve, even if only for our own survival.

A final factor we need to weigh is the growing divergence between what we think is happening in the classroom and what is actually taking place. Here I would like to turn to some work of John Goodlad (1977). Based upon his recent studies of schools in action, Goodlad suggests that there are actually five different curricula: *Ideal curriculum*, what scholars (like James Moffett) believe should be taught; *Formal curriculum*, what some controlling agency (like the state or the local district) has prescribed; *Perceived curriculum*, what teachers believe they are teaching in response to the needs of the pupils; *Operational curriculum*, what an observer would actually see being taught in the classroom; *Experiential curriculum*, what the students believe they are learning.

There are important differences among these five, of course, in the degree to which they are implemented and in the extent to which they agree with each other. To begin with, the scholar's recommendations are largely ignored by the classroom teacher, who finds them either too recondite or too unrealistic. The formal curriculum is often quietly subverted, the mimeographed curriculum guide filed in the bottom cabinet until evaluation time. Like Goodlad, Harry F. Wolcott (1977) provides evidence for the observation that projects which try to develop teacher-proof curricula fail because they fall into the hands of curriculum-proof teachers.

In an address to the 1979 convention of the Association for Supervision and Curriculum Development, as reported in the Association's *News Exchange*, John Goodlad (1979, pp. 1, 8) made this comment, based upon his study of schools:

> American teachers generally ignore state and district curriculum guides in planning classes, preferring to rely primarily on their own personal background and their sense of the interests and abilities of children in their classes.

After examining from an anthropological perspective the results of an attempt to impose an educational innovation upon reluctant teachers, Wolcott (1977, p. 151) reached this conclusion about the "ideational system" of teachers:

> Teachers want to retain the authority for instructional decisions, to be able to judge for themselves what is best in terms of students and instructional programs. They protect their autonomy by pointing to the need for flexibility and by insisting that they either be allowed to choose between options or else be left completely alone. The teacher must be free to decide what works and what does not.

The classroom observer often sees something quite different from the teacher's reports of what was planned or taught. Philip Cusick (1973), in his ethnographic study, *Inside High School*, has discouraging evidence that neither the perceived curriculum nor the operational curriculum makes any difference at all to the students in the classroom.

Goodlad's research suggests, then, that we need to bring those five curricula into closer convergence and respect the autonomy of classroom teachers, abandoning any attempts to impose an "ideal" or "formal" curriculum upon them.

Let me conclude this examination of past and present by summarizing what seem to be the implications of that examination, using again the rubric from the previous chapter for examining those changes: the process of developing the curriculum, its content, and the format by which the curriculum will be delivered.

*Process of Development*

1. The process should be simple, fast, inexpensive, and focused. It should not require teams of experts, long periods of development, and excessive funding. It should focus on the heart of the subject—what will later be explained as the mastery curriculum.
2. The process should take cognizance of and begin with the perceived curriculum—what is actually being taught. It will therefore provide for substantial contributions from the classroom teacher.
3. The process should result in the convergence of the ideal, the formal, and the perceived. It should not perpetuate the separation of these three forms of the curriculum.

*Curriculum Content*

1. The content of the written curriculum should be focused and restricted; the written curriculum should concern itself only with the heart of the subject, the so-called mastery elements.
2. The content should reflect a syncretic orientation, drawing from analyses of the four substantive orientations: the cognitive processes, the social setting, the subject itself, and the student. (The technological orientation emphasizes means, not substance.)
3. The content should make an adequate response to such external requirements as state mandates, standardized tests, and community expectations.
4. The content should be research-based, reflecting our best knowledge about the subject and the student.
5. The content should be comprehensive and articulated: All important skills and concepts should be included in a sequence that makes sense.

*Curriculum Format*

1. The format in which the curriculum is delivered to the teachers should be flexible, accommodating to a variety of teaching styles, and requiring no radical changes in teaching style.
2. The format should be usable and open, one that teachers will use and add to.

3. The format should readily accommodate computers and video devices.

Obviously the author supports a process of incremental change, and here the recommendation of Joseph Schwab (1969, pp. 14, 15) is most apposite. In recommending that curriculum be more aware of "the practical," he makes this observation:

> The practical arts begin with the requirement that existing institutions and existing practices be preserved and altered piecemeal, not dismantled and replaced. It is further necessary that changes be so planned and articulated with what remains unchanged that the functioning of the whole remains coherent and unimpaired. . . . The same requirements would hold for a practical program of improvement of education. It too would effect its changes in small progressions, in coherence with what remains unchanged and thus would require that we know *what is and what has been going on in American schools.* [Italics in original]

How we meet these requirements is the substance of the rest of this book.

# 3 A Process of Incremental Curriculum Development

What process can meet the criteria identified in the previous chapter? This chapter will present an overview of such a process, and succeeding chapters will discuss in greater detail the more important steps in implementing it. Figure 2 presents a planning calendar which lists the steps in order, indicates the participants, and suggests a schedule. The timing, obviously, will vary with the scope of the project and the resources available; the dates are intended only to suggest an average time commitment and to show that the essentials of the project can be completed within fifteen months.

1. Determine need; identify parameters, resources, and responsibilities. Either as a result of some administrative edict ("Coordinate that curriculum!") or out of your own sense of need, you decide to improve the teaching of English by strengthening the curriculum. You meet with the superintendent (or whoever is in charge of your school) to get answers to the following questions:

   a. What grade levels and areas of the curriculum will be included?

   b. How much money is available?

   c. How much time do we have?

   d. How much help do I get?

   We'll assume that all this happens toward the end of a school year. And the answers you get will be used to make your own, more detailed planning calendar.

2. Inform English teachers and solicit their cooperation.

   Note that it is suggested that this step be taken twice: in May, as soon as the project has been authorized; and again in September, because the teachers will probably have forgotten what you said in May. It is recommended that you send out a short notice something like this:

> I've been asked by the superintendent to take a fresh look at our English curriculum and determine if any improvements are needed. I expect to spend most of next school year working at this task. Even at this stage I know there will not be any radical changes in what or how we teach. I'll keep you fully informed at every step along the way. I'd appreciate whatever cooperation you can give me, and I promise to keep meetings to an absolute minimum.

3. Brief the district leadership about mastery theory, determining whether that theory will govern curriculum work. As explained in the next chapter, focused curriculum work is advocated which emphasizes only the so-called mastery part of the curriculum. The point here is that the adoption or rejection of that theory will clearly affect all that follows; therefore, the top administrators should be briefed early so that a decision can be made about the use of the mastery concept.

These first three planning and briefing steps can be taken before the school year ends. You can spend the summer reading and relaxing. Then, when the next school year begins, you set to work on the major developmental steps.

4. Select the task force, advisory council, and writing team. You'll need some help—and you want people to feel that this is not a one-person show. While the project should be kept simple, I have found that three groups are useful. The first is the "English Curriculum Task Force," a small working group that will do most of the planning and reviewing. Its membership should probably include the following:

   1. One or more department heads, depending upon the size of the district.
   2. One secondary principal.
   3. One elementary curriculum specialist.
   4. One administrator with districtwide curriculum responsibility.
   5. One English curriculum consultant.

The second group is the "English Curriculum Advisory Council." As noted in a later chapter, the main function of the advisory council is to provide you with a useful means of assessing community attitudes and expectations. The extent to which you use the group depends upon your own biases about such committees; the important thing is to be honest with them at the outset about their function and their authority. Its membership should include students, teachers, parents, and representatives of business and industry.

The final group is a small team of English teachers (one from each grade) who will be paid to do whatever writing needs to be done. They should be chosen for their knowledge of the subject and their ability to write clearly. They should be paid, preferably, by the job, not by time: "You'll get $500 when you deliver in September an acceptable product. Do the job where and when you prefer—but it must meet these specifications." If funds are unavailable it is possible to get the job done by volunteers—but it is strongly recommended that the writers be compensated. All three groups are selected in September—the task force first, the advisory council next, the writing team last. And the writing team should probably be selected from volunteers.

5. Collect and tally mapping data. As noted in Chapter 5, the work begins by finding out what is actually being taught—by mapping the existing curriculum. The process, explained fully in Chapter 5, should take about a month.

6. Develop preliminary versions of the content planning matrix. Use the mapping data to develop a first draft of a "Content Planning Matrix"—otherwise called a scope and sequence chart. Chapter 6 explains in detail how do this.

7. Evaluate the matrix and make appropriate modifications. This is one of the most important steps—and consequently should be done with great care. Allow three months for it, or you may wish to devote even more time to this step. You spend all that time making several careful analyses of the content planning matrix, to be sure that it represents the best possible plan for future curriculum work. How to undertake this evaluation is explained fully in Chapter 7.

8. Meet with teachers to revise the matrix and determine format of guides. During the next two months you hold several small group meetings with the teachers to accomplish two important tasks: (a) review with them the changes suggested for the planning matrix, to be sure that the changes are acceptable; and (b) solicit their suggestions about the format they find most useful.

My recommendations about this matter of format are explained in Chapter 11, but the teachers should have an opportunity to make suggestions here.

9. Prepare the writing team for writing course objectives. The final version of the content planning matrix is translated into lists of course objectives. As noted in Chapter 11, these are general learning objectives for the mastery curriculum. You will need to spend some time in May, reviewing with the writing team what they are expected to do—and how they are expected to do it.

10. Monitor the writing team. You will probably spend some time in the summer, monitoring the work of the writing team. As noted above, the team should preferably be paid by the job, not by the hour. They should not be required to sit in a hot curriculum office from 9 till 4; they should be able to work at their own pace in their own place. But they should be paid for successful performance of the task, not for the hours they spend. Although they should have this independence and will be accountable for final quality, you probably need to develop some system for evaluating their work during the formative stages.

11. Check course objectives against course offerings. Once the course objectives for each grade have been developed, you may then need to do a reverse kind of mapping, checking to ensure that courses are sequenced and offered in a way that ensures that students study all the mastery objectives. Special problems develop with variations such as elective and humanities courses; these are explained more fully in Chapters 12 and 14.

12. Determine plans for future development of materials. The final step is to take stock as to where you are and what still needs to be done. Depending upon available resources and apparent needs, you may decide to write mastery learning units a la Bloom, write student learning packages, develop staff training programs, work on other curriculum components, or just sit tight. These matters are also explained more fully in later chapters.

The process outlined above meets the criteria set. First, it is simple, fast, inexpensive, and focused. It takes only one academic year to implement. It requires no expensive teams of experts. And it focuses on the mastery elements. Second, it begins with the perceived curriculum and respects the autonomy of the classroom teacher. It does not impose a curriculum upon the teachers, but derives one from them. Finally, it brings together the ideal, the formal, and the perceived curricula by beginning with the perceived, adding essential elements of the formal, and refining the results by bringing to bear the research perspectives of the ideal.

# 4 The Mastery Curriculum

In discussing the curriculum development process recommended in the previous chapter, a preference was indicated for a focused curriculum, one that concerns itself centrally with what are called the mastery elements, and it was suggested that this identification of the mastery components should be one of the earliest steps in the process. This chapter offers a rationale for and fuller explanation of the mastery curriculum. It should be noted that there is an important distinction between the concept of the mastery curriculum, as I have developed it, and the theory of mastery learning, as Bloom and his students (Bloom, 1976; Block and Anderson, 1975) have described it.

The mastery curriculum, as will be explained more fully below, is that portion of any curriculum which is both essential and structured; it may be delivered through a mastery learning mode or through any of several other instructional methodologies. Mastery learning is an instructional system which, according to Bloom, can be applied to the entire curriculum. However, its emphasis on specific objectives, frequent assessment, and error remediation makes it inappropriate for all organic learning and for any integrated thematic units which would emphasize discovery and inductive learning.

This concept of a mastery curriculum developed out of the author's awareness of two significant weaknesses characterizing most curricular efforts of the past several decades. The first, as suggested earlier, is the single-dimension view of the discipline which asks curriculum practitioners to act like Procrustes. Thus the academic rationalists involved with much of Project English argued that the entire English curriculum should be structured in the Brunerian sense. They were followed by James Moffett and other romantic radicals who argued persuasively for an integrated "student-centered" curriculum emphasizing personal relevance and shaped according to the learner's developing ability to use symbols and make abstractions. (See, for example, Moffett and Wagner, 1976.) And now, in this period of privatistic conservatism, it seems as if the technocrats hold sway, showing us how to twist all of English so that it fits a mastery learning mode (for example, Block and Anderson, 1975).

The second weakness, which is perhaps related to the first, is what I choose to call curricular extravagance. It is a wasteful attempt to control through the written curriculum everything remotely concerned with communication. Thus it is extravagant, both in the older sense of "straying beyond limits or bounds," and in the contemporary sense of "giving to imprudent expenditure."

The mastery curriculum, then, is my attempt to eliminate these two weaknesses by viewing English through several perspectives and by focusing curriculum development efforts on only a certain portion of that curriculum. I begin by proposing that we analyze the discipline according to two dimensions: essentiality and structure. (Continued reference will be made to the field of English, although I believe the model can be applied to all major disciplines.)

Each discipline can be divided in terms of essentiality into learnings that are *basic* for all students and those that are *enrichment*. Basic learnings are those which, in the view of informed practitioners and scholars, are essential for all students to master; enrichment learnings are those which are not essential, even though they may be interesting to the student or intriguing to the scholar.

The second analysis is in terms of structure. Each discipline can be divided into learnings that are structured and nonstructured. Here a definition is more crucial. Structured learning, as used here, has these characteristics:

1. It requires careful sequencing; the learning of objective 3 depends upon the mastery of objectives 1 and 2.

2. It is best facilitated through careful planning; teaching objective 3 requires deliberate analysis of its component skills.

3. It results in measurable outcomes; a test can easily determine whether objective 3 has been mastered.

4. It is best mastered when its content is clearly delineated into discrete units or lessons; objective 3 can easily be set off from objective 4.

Nonstructured learning, on the other hand, embraces all those skills, concepts, and attitudes which can be mastered without such careful sequencing, planning, and delineation.

These two analyses yield four distinctly different areas of the curriculum, best illustrated thus:

ESSENTIALITY

| | | BASIC | ENRICHMENT |
|---|---|---|---|
| S T R U C T U R E | STRUCTURED | Mastery | Team-planned |
| | NONSTRUCTURED | Organic | Student-determined |

*The mastery curriculum* is that part of the curriculum which meets two important criteria: it is essential or basic for all students; it requires careful structuring for optimal learning. It is the part of the curriculum that best fits a mastery learning mode. It requires careful planning, frequent assessment, systematic organization, and district articulation. It probably can be learned best when objectives are clearly delineated in advance and when the teacher directs learning in a highly task-oriented fashion.

In my view the content of the English mastery curriculum should be influenced most strongly by the "cognitive processes" and "academic rationalism" orientations, and to a lesser degree by "social adaptation and reconstruction" and "personal relevance." Its design and delivery, however, will be directly shaped by the "curriculum as technology" orientation. The sequence of learning experiences in the mastery curriculum is determined primarily by what Posner and Strike (1976) call concept-related or learning related principles: In their terms, "concept-related sequences reflect the organization of the conceptual world" and "learning-related . . . sequences draw primarily on knowledge about the psychology of learning as a basis for curriculum development."

*The organic curriculum* is just as essential as the mastery curriculum but it is different in a crucial way: it is nonstructured. This means that it is best learned without careful planning and sequencing; it develops more organically without planned teacher intervention. It is best facilitated not by graded, structured units of study but by a sensitive teacher who responds to the emergent needs of the learner. I believe that most, if not all, of the affective goals of education are organic in this sense; they should not be programmed into structured curricula but should be nurtured by a responsive teacher. Thus it would be foolish to develop a third-grade unit in "enjoying reading." The enjoyment of reading should be cultivated in every unit, in every year.

I also believe that most of the development of oral language competence is more properly facilitated through an organic approach. The child comes to school knowing how to speak and needs only the support of a sensitive, caring teacher, not structured units in "conversing with friends."

Obviously the organic curriculum should be strongly influenced by a "personal relevance" orientation. What matters chiefly are the needs of the student as they emerge developmentally. There is no predetermined sequence; the sequence is dictated by the student's increasing command of the language and the developing ability to think abstractly.

*The team-planned curriculum* involves enrichment learnings that are not essential for all students—but that do require some minimal structuring. This term is used to suggest that this component of the curriculum is best planned by teams of teachers working out informal systems of coordination, simply to ensure that the enrichment learnings are not repeated—and also to guarantee that important elements of enrichment are in fact included for all who can profit from them.

It seems reasonable for the team-planned curriculum to be influenced by "academic rationalism" and "social adaptation and reconstruction" orientations since they seem to be orientations influencing much enrichment content of interest to teachers.

*The student-determined curriculum* is neither basic nor structured. It is that part of the curriculum which can be determined almost entirely by the student. It is a spontaneous curriculum which emerges from the interests (not the needs) of the student and is therefore most responsive to fashion and fad. While the same "personal relevance" orientation will be most influential here, an impact will also be made by the "social adaptation and reconstruction" orientation as students raise questions about current social problems.

Now I would argue that these distinctions are more than interesting theoretical speculations; they have important implications for the leader and the teacher. Some of the most important of these are:

1. The mastery curriculum is the curriculum with which school district curriculum specialists should be most concerned. Only the mastery curriculum needs careful delineation in scope and sequence charts and detailed development in curriculum guides. Since most district curriculum guides embrace all four areas, they are unnecessarily comprehensive and extravagant. Identifying the mastery curriculum will enable us to focus our efforts where such curriculum work will be most effective.

2. The mastery curriculum can become the accountable curriculum. Classroom teachers, led by district curriculum specialists and advised by subject-matter consultants, should identify the elements of the mastery curriculum. It thus becomes a consensus curriculum, and it then seems reasonable to hold teachers accountable for teaching it—but not to hold teachers accountable for the students' learning of it.

3. The mastery curriculum can readily be developed into mastery learning units which should ensure measurable student progress—but only the mastery curriculum should be shaped to fit this mold. The current interest in mastery learning should not lead us into the mistake of trying to force the organic curriculum into a mastery mode. I worry about people who write mastery learning units before they identify the mastery curriculum.

4. The mastery curriculum is the one that should determine the selection of textbooks. Teachers have been wisely skeptical of textbooks filled with inordinate amounts of content from the organic curriculum. The organic curriculum needs no textbook; in fact, the textbook may get in the way. But the mastery curriculum is often helped by a good textbook.

5. The organic curriculum should not be packaged, measured, or distorted by the heavy hand of instructional technologists. Instead, classroom teachers need systematic in-service work to help them foster organic learnings in natural ways on a continuing basis. The organic curriculum is just as important as the mastery curriculum (if not more so), but it should not be the concern of district curriculum guides.

6. The analysis suggests differential responsibility for development and implementation. District leaders take primary

responsibility for developing the mastery curriculum with substantial input by classroom teachers. The classroom teacher becomes responsible for fostering the objectives of the organic curriculum. Teams of teachers informally plan the team-planned curriculum, and students identify the important elements of the student-determined curriculum.

Figure 3 attempts to summarize the salient features of these four different curricula and makes it clear that the differences are both real and important.

Two questions have frequently been raised in districts where I have used the theory in curricular consultation. One that is often raised is, "How much time should the mastery curriculum take?" The answer, obviously, will vary both with local decisions and other important factors such as grade level and student ability. In general, the mastery curriculum should never require more than 60 to 75 percent of the total time available, leaving sufficient time for the other aspects.

In working with several school districts I have discovered that about 20 percent of the objectives included in their curriculum guides could be more wisely allocated to the team-planned component and about 20 percent to the organic component. The advantages of such focusing should be readily apparent.

The second question often raised is, "What are your own recommendations as to what elements belong in the mastery curriculum for English?" It has been noted before that affective goals and the development of oral language are more properly part of the organic curriculum. Other than those general positions, I would be reluctant to impose my own biases here because I advocate a consensus process that grants most authority to the classroom teacher.

If this analysis of structure and essentiality makes sense, then how can it be used in the curriculum planning process? The following sequence of steps is suggested:

1. The instructional leader makes copies of this chapter and sends them to district administrators and curriculum workers, suggesting that a meeting be held to discuss the implications of the theory for future district curriculum development and in-service training.

2. At the meeting, the ideas are thoroughly examined and argued. Those attending may wish to modify the theory or restate it in their own words. The group may, of course,

decide to reject the notion and continue their curriculum work without further reference to the theory.

3. If the leadership group accepts the theory (or their own modification of it), it becomes the basis of future curriculum work. District leaders agree that district curriculum development will focus only on mastery elements.

4. Any individual or group doing curriculum work for the district is thoroughly briefed on the theory and is expected either to accept it as the basis for that work or to present cogent reasons to the contrary.

If that kind of agreement is reached, future curriculum development is likely to be more focused, less extravagant, and more eclectic in orientation.

# 5 Curriculum Mapping

As noted previously, the curriculum development process should start with the perceived curriculum, respecting the autonomy of the classroom teacher and reflecting the consensus of the faculty as to what should be taught. Such a consensus obviously is not achieved through commands issued from the top down or through more stringent controls emanating from the formal curriculum; it should emerge from the bottom up, through a systematic involvement of the classroom teacher. Rather than write one more curriculum guide which will again be ignored, we begin by finding out what is actually being taught. This process of discerning the perceived or taught curriculum is sometimes called curriculum mapping. (As far as can be determined, the term was first used and explained by Fenwick W. English in 1978.)

## Mapping the Curriculum

How do you map the curriculum? The answer depends upon the scope of your responsibility, the size of your school and district, and the resources available to you. The most reliable way would be to observe (or have trained colleagues observe) every teacher, every week, with every class. Such extensive observation is obviously not feasible. You could also ask teachers to submit unit and end-of-year examinations, texts, lesson plans, and teaching materials, which you would then analyze. This process is probably too time-consuming and might make teachers feel anxious and resentful. You can ask the students what they have studied, but you probably will not get valid data. ("We never had that stuff.")

The most practical solution of the problem of mapping is to survey the teachers. There are some obvious limitations here, of course. The process will take time. Teachers may misunderstand the instructions. Some will probably be suspicious, despite your assurances. And the information you get will be no more useful than that from any self-report of behavior. But it's probably the best compromise. And following certain common-sense steps will increase the validity of the data.

First you have to decide which grade levels you need to map. The answer will depend, of course, on how your school district is organized and the extent of the curriculum project. Let us suppose for purposes of illustration that you are the high school department head in a district which uses this grade-level organization: K–5, 6–8, 9–12. You have been asked to strengthen the 6–12 curriculum. You have two choices:

1. With the cooperation of elementary faculty, map the K–12 curriculum, work out cooperatively any serious problems of repetition or omission between the elementary and middle school curricula, and then focus your efforts on 6–12.

2. Map the 6–12 curriculum only, with the realization that the K–5 program should be mapped at a later date and problems of overlap and omission dealt with at that time.

The second decision is on the number of separate maps you will need. If your system has three clearly defined tracks (gifted, slow, and all the rest), then you will probably make three maps, beginning with the group in which you are most interested. If you sense that one basic curriculum is in operation, with teachers responding to individual difference in an ad hoc fashion, then you probably can do with one map.

## Deciding Which Areas to Map

You then decide how many separate areas of the English curriculum you wish to map. (The term *area* is used here to designate the major subdivisions of a discipline.) Your answer to this question depends upon your assessment of these two issues: Which terms will communicate most clearly to the teachers? Which sort of division will yield most useful data? My recommendation is that you map these eight areas, keeping in mind that separate mapping does not necessarily mean separate teaching:

| | |
|---|---|
| Reading and study skills | Word study and vocabulary |
| Literature and the media | Speaking and listening |
| Composition | Critical and creative thinking |
| Grammar and language | Spelling, punctuation, and usage |

You then meet with teachers in small groups to clarify further the concept of the mastery curriculum, explain the mapping project, discuss the terminology, answer their questions, and solicit their suggestions. In the meeting you probably will want to make these points:

1. The mapping project derives from a respect for teacher autonomy.

2. There is no hidden agenda. The data will not be used to evaluate teachers, departments, or schools. The survey forms need not be signed; you will assign teachers a code number (which you alone will be able to identify) in order to ensure complete returns.

3. The delineation of separate areas of the English curriculum is designed to yield useful mapping data, not to suggest that the curriculum be thus fragmented. You know that many teachers integrate these skills; for purposes of the project, they should report them separately.

4. The mapping project is concerned with the mastery elements only. You do not believe that the organic curriculum needs to be mapped, and you are not concerned at this point with either kind of enrichment.

5. The degree of specificity used in reporting mapping information will depend somewhat upon the area of the curriculum and the teacher's perspective. In general you prefer that teachers identify major skills and concepts, not narrowly defined learning objectives.

6. The data will be collated and subject to further review by consultants, administrators, and an advisory council. Teachers will be informed about such developments.

7. You want information at this stage as to what is taught; later you will solicit their recommendations about any changes that might be made.

You then leave with them a "Curriculum Mapping Form" on which they will report the general skills, concepts, and units taught. You suggest a deadline by which the forms should be returned and note that you hope for a complete return so that the data yielded will give an accurate picture of the "taught" curriculum. Every teacher, of course, should receive one form for each grade taught. You have a choice here as to the design and content of mapping forms. You may wish to use a simpler, open-ended form like that shown in Figure 4, which lists only the major areas of the discipline and shows how one eleventh grade teacher might have completed the form. Or you may wish to use a more detailed set of forms, using one page for each area of the curriculum and analyzing that area into its component strands. For example, your page for the grammar and language area might include these strands: word classes or parts of speech; sentence parts; sentence patterns and types; phonology; morphology; dialect study; language history.

When the forms are returned, you and the task force begin to collate and analyze the data. Here you would use what I call a Content Planning Matrix (or a scope and sequence chart)—an important document which is explained more fully in the next chapter. When that analysis has been completed you should have a reasonably accurate picture of the "taught" curriculum.

# 6 Building A Content Planning Matrix

The content planning matrix, as used here, is generally similar to what is usually called a scope and sequence chart. I prefer my own term because I believe it suggests more accurately the emphasis, form, and use of the document. It emphasizes content, not the methodology of English. It is a matrix in form, presenting an array of cells derived from the intersection of grade levels and curricular strands. And it provides a basis for future planning by both curriculum worker and teacher.

### Developing a Content Planning Matrix

Several important points should be made regarding the form of the content planning matrix before explaining how it is developed. First, the grade levels are intended only as a convenient representation of developmental levels; they do not mandate fixed progression. It is quite easy to use the graded matrix as the basis of a nongraded or individualized program. Second, the eight areas of the English curriculum which were used in gathering mapping data are further analyzed into their component strands as a means of achieving greater clarity and facilitating use. How this analysis is performed will be explained later. The point here is that identifying separate areas and related component strands for purposes of analysis does not necessarily mean that units of study will be thus fragmented. A later chapter suggests several ways of developing integrated units and interdisciplinary courses.

Next, it is recommended that the items entered in the cells of the matrix should be general skills and concepts, not specific learning objectives which will later be derived from the general skills and concepts.

A few examples will clarify this matter. It is sufficient for the matrix to indicate that the concept of *noun* is taught in seventh grade; the matrix need not provide such details as "defines noun, discriminates between proper and common nouns, uses nouns in sentences." And the matrix might indicate that in the area of composition, the process essay is taught in grade nine, without specifying such detailed objectives as "begins essay effectively, identifies process, uses chronological order, defines terms," and so on. The use of general skills and concepts results in a more usable matrix, one that is not cluttered with confusing detail.

Finally, the items entered in the matrix represent where a particular skill or concept should receive primary and systematic emphasis. Such an entry does not preclude either informal introduction at an earlier level or thorough review at a later level. For example, indicating that the concept of *noun* is to be taught at grade seven does not prevent a teacher in grade five or six from explaining the concept briefly and using it informally in lessons about language; nor does it mean that the term need not be reviewed at a later date. It means only that the concept will receive primary and systematic emphasis at the level indicated.

## Strands as a Starting Point

How do you make the content planning matrix? With the help of the task force you begin by making eight charts, one for each area of the English curriculum. On each chart, list across the top the grade levels to be included. Down the left-hand side of the chart, list the component strands of that particular area. You can determine which strands to use either by making your own deductive analysis of the area or by inductively deriving them from a scanning of the returns. The sample form in Figure 5 shows the strands identified for the grammar-language study, and how part of the mapping data would be reported. You may choose how you wish to represent data from the several schools being surveyed. If numerous schools are participating in the project and you are uninterested in making differentiations by school, you can simply group and tally together all the data received. If you are surveying only two or three schools, you may wish to make a separate column for each school, as shown in Figure 5. Or you could use a color code to represent data from different schools. Note that the matrix at this stage is inclusive, not focused. For example, in the evaluation process described next, the strand "language history" might be moved to the "team-planned" curriculum.

With the forms prepared, you can begin collating the data submitted in the mapping project. With the assistance of the task force (or with the help of a secretary) you enter on the chart, grade by grade and area by area, the data derived from the mapping forms. At this stage you should not worry about repetitions or omissions. Those problems will be dealt with in the review and evaluation process described in the next chapter.

# 7 Evaluating and Modifying the Content Planning Matrix

With the preliminary version of the content planning matrix in hand, you are ready with the assistance of others to review the taught curriculum in order to determine where improvements, additions, and deletions may be needed. Such a review should be thorough because the results will become the basis for future curriculum development. The evaluation is based upon the five general criteria for content identified in Chapter 1:

1. *Focus.* The content of the written curriculum should be focused and restricted; the written curriculum should concern itself only with the heart of the subject—the mastery elements.

2. *Orientation.* The content of the curriculum should reflect a syncretic orientation, drawing from analyses of the four substantive orientations.

3. *Response to external requirements.* The content of the curriculum should make an adequate response to external requirements such as state mandates, standardized tests, and community expectations.

4. *Research basis.* The content of the curriculum should be research-based, reflecting our best knowledge about the subject and the student.

5. *Comprehensiveness and articulation.* The content of the curriculum should be comprehensive and articulated; all important skills and concepts should be included in a sequence that makes sense.

The specific evaluation issues to be considered in such a review are listed in Figure 6 under the five general criteria. Each will be discussed briefly here; a more extensive analysis of certain of the issues is offered in later chapters. The discussion that follows is organized in terms of the agent responsible, not the logical categories.

## Evaluation by Leader and Task Force

The instructional leader, assisted by the task force, begins with evaluation of the mapping data in terms of the following issues:

1. Are only mastery elements included and organic and enrichment components excluded? This first issue is concerned with focus. As noted in Chapter 3, the objective is to achieve economy of effort, so that only mastery elements become the concern of district leaders. You therefore should delete from the planning matrix any skills or concepts that seem to belong in the organic or enrichment curricula, keeping a record of any changes made.

My preference is for the instructional leader to apply the principle of parsimony: When in doubt, leave it out. Teachers are inclined to believe everything they teach is "basic" and are reluctant to omit a concept, no matter how special it might seem to a disinterested critic. The result is a swollen mastery curriculum that causes teachers to try to cover too much content. I think we would do much better to teach a few things well.

2. Does the content reflect a syncretic orientation, drawing from analyses of the four substantive orientations? This is an important concern that requires careful thought. The easiest check is to make certain that the content adequately represents the subject itself; the form of the matrix and the inclinations of subject-trained teachers both suggest that the subject will be adequately covered. The cognitive processes orientation will also probably be in evidence, since cognitive processes in my view include two of the so-called basics of English—reading and composing. However, I have included "critical thinking" and "creative thinking" in the planning matrix as a reminder that there are some important problem-solving skills which need to be emphasized. It is somewhat more difficult to make certain that the curriculum adequately responds to student personal relevance and to the society. All these matters are dealt with more fully in a later chapter.

3. Are basic competencies mandated by state or local district provided for? Chapter 9 explains more fully how such provisions can readily be made. It is sufficient to note here the importance of this analysis. If such mandates exist, the curriculum must respond to them.

4. Is there a satisfactory match between the elements of the curriculum and items included in standardized tests used by the district? Despite the complaints of classroom teachers and the

criticisms of scholars (see, for example, "Common Sense and Testing in English," by Alan Purves and the Task Force on Measurement and Evaluation in the Study of English, 1975), such tests will continue to be used, and teachers and schools unfortunately will be judged by the results. You should therefore secure copies of the tests in general use, along with the examiner's manual, to identify what is included test by test. If discrepancies turn up, there are two obvious responses. You can find another test, one that corresponds more closely to the taught curriculum. (One of the best sources for reviewing tests in English is Oscar K. Buros's *English Tests and Reviews*, 1975). Or you can change the curriculum by adding mastery content at appropriate grade levels. It might be noted here that you should find fewer discrepancies than perhaps anticipated. After reviewing the grammar content of eleven widely used standardized tests, Gary A. Sutton (1976, p. 40) observes, "The obvious conclusion to be drawn from the data is that grammar terminology per se is a very minor aspect of standardized tests in English."

5. Within a given area of the English curriculum, does the vertical sequence of skills and concepts from grade to grade seem to follow a coherent, acceptable plan? Here as leader you should examine a given area of the English curriculum along its continuum (from grades seven through twelve, for example) to determine if there is an acceptable plan. It would probably be unwise at this juncture to impose some sequence on the taught curriculum, since there is no inherent superiority in any given sequence. In an article identifying seventeen kinds of sequencing principles, Posner and Strike (1976, p. 665) make this observation:

> The question of how content should be sequenced or ordered has been the subject of educational debates for at least 70 years. . . . However, no satisfactory answer has been developed, and no adequate prescription is expected in the near future. . . . We have very little information, based on hard data, regarding the consequence of alternative content sequences and will need a good deal more research effort before we are able to satisfactorily suggest how content should be sequenced.

There are two important concerns at this stage. The first is to detect problems of sequence likely to interfere with learning—for example, teaching the kinds of sentences (using a typology based on kinds of clauses) before teaching the kinds of clauses. The second, as noted below, is to be sure that the sequence reflects the best knowledge about child and language development.

6. Are all important skills and concepts included, with no significant omissions? Here the leader needs to exercise critical judgment in reviewing the returns to be sure that there are no major omissions.

7. Are skills and concepts appropriately reinforced without excessive repetition? This question also requires judgment. How much reinforcement is needed? Is the reinforcement accompanied by increasing depth of treatment, so that there is a kind of Brunerian spiral?

8. At a given grade level, do the several areas of the curriculum exhibit complementarity, where such complementarity seems appropriate? This analysis examines the fit or match between areas of the English curriculum at a given grade level, to determine whether some realignment of elements might bring about greater complementarity between areas. For example, the study of American dialects might be shifted from grade ten to grade eleven to complement the study of American literature. As pointed out in a later chapter, there is no inherent virtue in an integrated English language arts curriculum; however, it makes sense to align major elements in order to facilitate integration where it is desirable.

9. Is there sufficient uniformity among schools at the same level to ensure efficiency and consistency of results? Experience leads me to believe that superintendents worry too much about the need for all junior high or high schools to follow essentially the same program. I think they worry unduly about parents' making invidious comparisons between schools. While I think such fears are exaggerated, and while I value school autonomy, it seems reasonable to expect some degree of uniformity in the major components of the mastery curriculum from school to school. Such general uniformity will minimize problems for students transferring from one school to another and should facilitate the sharing of materials.

10. From grade to grade, is there a reasonable balance (considering the students' maturity) in terms of the number of important concepts and skills to be learned? This analysis is performed by examining the mapping data along the vertical dimension, to make certain that the amount of work represented suggests a reasonable balance in terms of student maturity. Special attention should be paid to the middle school years as this review is undertaken. Many teachers experienced in working with middle school learners suggest that these younger adolescents cannot deal effectively with undue academic pressure.

You can probably perform these analyses soon after all the data have been collated. In each case, of course, you should record on the draft version of the matrix any major changes that have been made.

## Evaluation by Leader and Consultant

The revised matrix should then be reviewed from the standpoint of research.

11. Does the taught curriculum reflect the best available research about the learner and the subject of English?

For this review it is recommended that a consultant be used, if only to gain the advantage of an objective critique. The consultant can also review other evaluations you have made of the data. Chapter 10 summarizes the important research findings related to this key issue, to facilitate your or the consultant's review. Again, a careful record should be made of any changes resulting from this analysis.

## Evaluation by Leader and Advisory Council

The final review is designed to ensure that the taught curriculum responds adequately to the reasonable expectations of parents, local employers, and the general community. For such a review, a twelve-to-fifteen-member advisory council should be useful, as noted previously. The advisory council should be thoroughly briefed at every stage of the process and should be fully informed at every stage of major developments. However, I suggest that their major contributions should be made toward the end of the review process. My bias here is clear: I do not believe that instructional leaders should abdicate their responsibility by asking a lay council at the outset, "What do you think we should teach in English?" Neither do I believe that citizens should be excluded from the review process; their reasonable recommendations should be heard. Note the important word *reasonable*. I believe that any recommendations that fly in the face of our knowledge of the learner and the subject, or that reflect racist or sexist biases, should be politely rejected. It is obviously important that such ground rules be made clear at the outset so that the advisory council accurately understands the scope of its authority.

Throughout this entire process you as the instructional leader have played an active role, bringing to bear at every stage your critical judgment—but making only those changes that seem essential. The revised matrix is then submitted to the teachers

for their final review and it should be presented in a form that is
easy to interpret and use. There is no need in the revised form of
the matrix for tally marks or school identifications. A message
like the following is attached to the document:

> The enclosed planning matrix summarizes your own and
> current practices, as they have been refined and modified after
> several reviews. Please examine the matrix carefully. You will be
> able to discuss any concerns at a meeting to be held on _____ .

That series of meetings gives you a chance to clarify matters,
explain the reasons for changes, and work out any compromises
that seem necessary. The final version of the planning matrix then
becomes the basis for further planning and development.

Figure 7 shows how the revised content planning matrix might
look for the area of composition. The intention here is not to
suggest that this is an ideal composition program, only to illustrate
some matters of form and content. Note, first, that the several
strands are listed at the left. Remember that such a listing does not
necessarily mean that these must be taught as separate units. Also
observe that the entries are stated in rather general terms; all that
matters is that they communicate the general nature of the skill or
concept to be mastered. Finally, as the matrix shows, there need
not be one concept per cell. Some cells may be blank; some may
have two or more entries.

# 8 Developing the Syncretic English Curriculum

As noted in Chapter 1, the ideal English curriculum as developed by curriculum theorists and language scholars has most often reflected one of the four substantive orientations identified by Eisner: academic rationalism, cognitive processes, personal relevance, and social adaptation and reconstruction. Such a single orientation, in retrospect, seems to have resulted in an undesirable narrowing of the curriculum and has increased teacher resistance to the ideal curriculum. The argument in this chapter, therefore, is that the English curriculum of the eighties should be characterized by a syncretic orientation, drawing appropriately from all four basic sources.

Such an orientation, I believe, would avoid the two weaknesses of the single-perspective curriculum. First, it should result in a curriculum that is likely to be more effective in achieving more comprehensive goals of English education. An appropriate emphasis on cognitive processes should ensure that basic reasoning and communicating skills are being developed. A concern for the social orientation of the curriculum should result in a curriculum that helps students understand and cope with the world of which they are a part. Academic rationalism provides a warrant for including important content from the fields of language and literature, which require no utilitarian justification. And an appropriate emphasis on personal relevance should result in a curriculum that is perceived as more relevant and interesting to the student. In short, the English curriculum will be strongest when it addresses comprehensive goals.

Such a syncretic orientation should also seem to be more appealing and sensible to the classroom teacher. As observed in Chapter 1, classroom teachers tend to be syncretic in practice. Their training probably has provided them with a basic orientation toward the importance of the discipline. Their experience has shown them the value of teaching the cognitive processes. They feel under pressure from the community and the state to teach socially derived learnings. And they know they can motivate

47

students best with content and activities that are personally relevant. They therefore will commit themselves more strongly to a curriculum that comprehensively responds to their instructional needs, rather than one that insists on a single orientation.

There is, of course, an obvious danger in such a syncretic curriculum: it could easily become too ambitious in scope, resulting in a lack of both focus and depth. The way to avoid this danger is for the instructional leader and the task force to exercise due control over the scope of the mastery curriculum, to ensure that it is not excessively ambitious.

Both objectives—ensuring that the curriculum is sufficiently syncretic, and controlling the scope of the mastery curriculum—can be attained through a systematic evaluation that uses the following processes:

1. The instructional leader and the task force should review the comprehensive criteria for a syncretic English curriculum listed in Figure 8.

2. They should record their individual responses to each criterion, choosing one of the following options: (a) this criterion is accepted and should be reflected primarily in the mastery curriculum, (b) this criterion is accepted but should be reflected primarily in the organic curriculum, (c) this criterion is accepted but should be reflected primarily in the team-planned curriculum, or (d) this criterion is not accepted.

3. Individual responses should be tallied. The leader and the task force should then focus their attention on the criteria accepted for the mastery curriculum, discussing their differences openly and attempting to reach a consensus on mastery criteria.

4. They should then apply the generally accepted mastery criteria in evaluating the planning matrix, adding units where omissions and weaknesses are noted.

5. Finally, the leader and the task force should review the planning matrix to ensure that it is not unduly swollen. One simple method is to estimate the number of weeks required for the average student at a given grade level to learn the mastery content. My recommendation is that the mastery units should not require more than twenty-seven weeks of work, approximately three-fourths of the total time available. At least one-fourth of the year should be available for remediation and enrichment.

If time permits, it would probably be desirable to set up a series of meetings for all English teachers, to give them an opportunity to discuss the criteria. Such sessions should result in lively exchanges about the goals of English—but probably will not produce a consensus. The instructional leaders and the task force will have to exercise their best professional judgment and make a decision, so that the curriculum project does not bog down in unproductive argument about the goals of English.

Such a process will result in a planning matrix that is sufficiently comprehensive and syncretic, without being unduly diffuse or superficial.

# 9 How to Provide for Mandated Competencies: Checking on the "Basics"

At the time of this writing, thirty-seven states had passed or were considering some form of competency-based education. While the slogan is variously interpreted, in general the legislation requires local school districts to undertake the following actions:

1. State in measurable terms the specific competencies which students should master before they are graduated.
2. Revise the school curriculum so that courses of study directly address those competencies.
3. Develop tests to measure those competencies.
4. Provide remediation for students who do not pass the tests, and award diplomas only when such competencies have been mastered.

While such notions seem reasonable enough, there is a danger that these ideas, mindlessly applied, may have deleterious effects on the English curriculum and English instruction, since the thrust of competency-based education is to emphasize both the measurable and the utilitarian. Here the author concurs with the reservations expressed by educators attending four regional conferences on competency-based education held under the auspices of the National Institute of Education in 1977. A summary report of the conference (Miller, 1978, p. 9) noted the concern thus:

> Much of the legislation specifically mentions the basic skills of reading, writing, and computing at minimum levels of proficiency, and life skills such as filling out forms, balancing checkbooks, and reading labels. Concern was expressed that the curriculum would be robbed of much of its richness if disproportionate amounts of resources are deployed into teaching minimum skills. Educators often pointed out that only those things that can be measured may receive attention, stressing the result of too much emphasis on those skills which are easily tested may cause neglect of other important objectives.

While I have strong reservations about competency-based education, there are three reasons that convince me of the need to make a positive response to such mandates. First, they grow out of a legitimate concern: all of us want students to become more competent. Second, it would seem foolhardy to ignore them, since most legislation and policy guidelines suggest some form of teacher accountability. And we cannot wait until this fad follows other ill-conceived innovations by quietly passing away; laws once passed are not quickly amended or repealed.

The only reasonable choice, then, is to develop a curriculum that includes provisions for competencies without focusing solely on the measurable and the utilitarian. This goal can be accomplished if we first understand that such mandated competencies tend to be of two quite different sorts: general competencies and applied competencies. A general competency, as the term is used here, is a cognitive skill, such as reading or writing, that is not restricted to a specific task or type of material. Thus, two of the "Basic Competencies in Reading" identified by the Vermont Department of Education (Kenney et al., 1977, p. 6) are general ones:

> Given unfamiliar material, the student will demonstrate ability to get pronunciation and meaning of new words by using word attack skills, structural analysis, and context.
>
> Given personally chosen material, the student will read aloud with clarity and emphasis, informally, to a small group.

On the other hand, an applied competency is any skill brought to bear on a specific task or kind of material. Thus, these two "Reading/Writing Life Competencies" identified by the New Mexico State Department of Education (n.d.) are applied: "The student will be able to read and comprehend a driver instructional manual"; and "The student will be able to write a 'job wanted' ad."

The two kinds of competencies impose quite different demands upon the curriculum. The general competencies of English are probably represented in the planning matrix by the several component strands. The instructional leader simply needs to ascertain that the horizontal 7–12 development of that strand provides for adequate emphasis of that general competency.

The applied competencies, on the other hand, are quite a different matter and require a different planning strategy. The following process is suggested:

First, the instructional leader and the task force should review all the applied competencies mandated by state or local authorities and categorize them according to the area of the curriculum—reading, writing, and so on.

They should then review the applied competencies for a given area and group them according to the specific learning skills required. To illustrate, the New Mexico State Department of Education (n.d.) list of "Reading/Writing Life Competencies" contains a total of forty-six competencies. Twenty-five of the forty-six are reading competencies, presented in the publication apparently in random order. However, a close analysis of the competencies suggests that they can be grouped into four different types, paraphrased below for the sake of brevity and clarity:

1. Competencies requiring the ability to comprehend informative prose presented in a standard format—the ability to read a driver's manual, a statement of voting rights, a procedure for reporting a lost credit card, information about available social services, a statement on the legal rights of individuals, a consumer credit contract.

2. Competencies requiring the ability to comprehend informative prose presented in a special format—the ability to read want ads, telephone directory, department store directory, radio and television schedules, food labels, recipes, clothing labels.

3. Competencies requiring the ability to comprehend special nonverbal symbols—the ability to read charts and graphs, maps, safety signs, transportation schedules.

4. Competencies requiring the ability to read critically—the ability to distinguish fact from opinion in a newspaper report or editorial.

The grouping clearly suggests four brief, focused instructional units: reading practical information, reading special forms, reading special symbols, reading the newspaper critically. These unit topics or titles would then be placed in an appropriate cell in the planning matrix: grade ten, reading. It is recommended that such applied competencies should be taught immediately prior to the time of assessment, since such very specific skills are easily forgotten. Since the New Mexico tests are given in grade ten, the applied skills should also be taught in grade ten, during the month prior to the test administration.

The final step in the planning process would be to write mastery learning units based upon those applied competencies. Chapter 15 explains how such units can be written. It should be emphasized that the teacher will probably get better results by teaching the competencies directly through a focused unit, rather than relying on an "incidental" approach or integrated unit.

Such a process enables us to make specific and adequate provisions for applied competencies without distorting or trivializing the entire curriculum. Note also that the process recommended here is quite distinct from so-called teaching for the test. I believe it is both ethical and prudent to teach units of study focused on the specific skills that will be measured in a forthcoming test. It is obviously unethical to drill students on test items taken from that test.

# 10 Using Research Knowledge to Improve the Teaching of English

One of the most important steps in evaluating the content planning matrix is to ensure that the selection and placement of mastery content is in accord with the current knowledge about the learner, the language, and the subject. In making such an assessment the instructional leader will probably encounter two kinds of responses which might interfere. On the one hand, there are many professor-types like the author (and some teachers) who uncritically accept any research finding and use it to attack their adversaries and impress their colleagues. The phrase falls easily from our lips at every possible juncture: "According to the research . . . ." On the other hand there are those at the other extreme, mostly classroom teachers, who cling to unsupported biases even in the face of conclusive findings that challenge such biases. They respond, "I don't care what the research says; I just know that my students write better because I teach them diagraming."

What we are after, I believe, is an informed and reflective personal knowing that Michael Polanyi (1966, p. 16) calls the "tacit dimension." His comments here seem especially apposite to those who would understand classrooms:

> It brings home to us that it is not looking at things, but by dwelling in them, that we understand their joint meaning. . . . An unbridled lucidity can destroy our understanding of complex matters.

Such an informed and reflective personal knowing comes about from the lived experience of teaching English—and the constant checking of perceptions derived therefrom against the findings of good research.

For this reason, the following pages include several summaries of major findings that seem especially relevant to curriculum and instruction in secondary English. Space is provided below each citation so that teachers can add new evidence as it is developed, and there is also space at the end of each group for adding new findings that seem important. Such summaries can be used in three ways:

The first is in the evaluation of the matrix. Here the instructional leader should review the matrix area by area, checking against the relevant research summary. Any major discrepancies between what the matrix records and what the research suggests should be noted for further review with the classroom teachers.

The second use is in organizing instructional seminars around the findings in a given area. Thus, a seminar might be held early in the year on the topic of "What Research and Informed Practice Say about the Teaching of Composition." Teachers would be expected to review the research summary and be prepared to participate actively in the seminar. Such a seminar might begin with the instructional leader asking for teachers to note any recent evidence or new findings. The leader can then open a discussion of the findings, asking teachers first to indicate their degree of acceptance and to comment on how they see the findings affecting their own teaching. They should also be encouraged, of course, to share their own successful practices.

The third use is to add the research summaries to the English notebook, as suggested before, so that they are at hand when teachers organize units or plan lessons. Here again the teacher is encouraged to add both information and reactions, so that the summaries become a compendium of one's informed and reflective personal knowledge.

There are some cautions and reservations about the quality and application of these findings. First, they are drawn from reviews of research carried out by scholars whom the author respects, but the original research studies have not been personally reviewed. Also, while the generalizations noted are supported by the findings of several studies which the reviewer considered to be satisfactorily designed and implemented, they are not to be perceived as final conclusions regarding the teaching of English. It is possible that future studies may reveal contrary findings. The findings are presented here as tentative generalizations that reflect current knowledge about the teaching of English. And while I believe that they should be influential in informing present practice, I consider it even more essential for instructional leaders to carry out their own continuing reviews of the research, to inform teachers about new developments, and to involve teachers in synthesizing reliable research findings with their tacit knowledge.

## Research Findings: Oral Language Development

1. Experience, thought, and language are interactive variables. "What is learned about the structure of the language influences the ways new experiences are stored and meanings are expressed. With increasing cognitive capacities for perceiving there are corresponding modifications in the child's language such that they become closer approximations of the formal language structures employed by the adult" (Di Vesta and Palermo, 1974, p. 69).

2. Although it has been generally established that the basic structures used by adults to generate their sentences can be found in the grammar of nursery school children, syntactic development continues well into later childhood and even adolescence (Di Vesta and Palermo, 1974).

3. Older children typically experience difficulty with the following syntactic elements: comprehension of the passive sentence; sentence constructions involving *ask/tell* followed by a pronoun; connectives such as *because, but, although;* the word *or* (Di Vesta and Palermo, 1974).

4. Phonological, syntactic, and semantic levels of analysis are highly interrelated (Di Vesta and Palermo, 1974).

5. "The interpretation of the effects of departures from standard English on cognitive ability has come to be delineated in the deficit-difference issue: advocates of the deficit position suggest that nonstandard English is related to cognitive impairment, while those advocating the difference position interpret the role of nonstandard English in cognitive ability as inconsequential. . . . Despite the impressive array of scholars and arguments presented on both sides of this issue, there is little empirical evidence based on investigations which directly compare predictions from the two models or directly test the deficiency-difference issue as alternative hypotheses" (Di Vesta and Palermo, 1974, pp. 91, 93).

6. Adolescents can construct contrary-to-fact propositions, can reason with abstract concepts, and can conceptualize their own and others' thoughts (Allen and Brown, 1976).

7. The adolescent understands the social significance of individual dialects and develops feelings accordingly (Allen and Brown, 1976).

8. Social class differences appear as adolescents participate in social class routines, especially verbal routines (Allen and Brown, 1976).

9. Children in early teens demonstrate normal adult competence in referential communication (Allen and Brown, 1976).

10. "There is evidence that seems to suggest that our patterns of instruction can inhibit learning and development. Whether or not we can actually teach communication is perhaps moot, but there seems to be no question concerning our ability to model desirable communication behaviors, reinforce them and offer feedback, shape roles, and structure experiences in which learning can occur" (Allen and Brown, 1976, p. 63).

11. The use of language laboratories in presenting behavior modification drills can be a help to adults in gaining greater phonological and syntactic control (Allen and Brown, 1976).

12. "Many linguists and language researchers have argued that the difference between the linguistically sophisticated and the linguistically immature is not so much the awareness of correct and incorrect usage but rather the general knowledge of a wide range of language varieties and adequate contact with the varieties most characteristic of school instruction. Many experiments and tests indicate that it is far more fruitful to expand the student's language repertory than it is to 'correct' the language he uses in his daily life" (Bordie, 1971, p. 85).

13. Language can be seen as having seven functions: instrumental (getting things done); regulatory (controlling others' behavior); interactional (maintaining relationships); personal (expressing personality); imaginative (creating a world); informative (conveying information); heuristic (finding things out). Teachers should help students develop and extend the functions for which they use oral language and pay attention to the functions of written language (Page and Pinnell, 1979).

14.

15.



16.



## Research Findings: The Teaching of Listening

1. Listening can be taught: Students who experience structured lessons on listening skills achieve better scores than those who do not (Devine, 1978).

2. Students spend approximately half their time in classrooms listening and almost half of their waking hours in listening (Wolvin and Coakley, 1979).

3. A review of theoretical analyses of listening suggests that listening skills can be conveniently grouped into five types: appreciative listening, discriminative listening, comprehensive listening, therapeutic or empathic listening, critical listening (Wolvin and Coakley, 1979).

4. Dialect users seem to have no difficulty in comprehending standard English (Marten, 1978).

5. A slow rate of presentation seems beneficial to young, verbally disadvantaged children (Marten, 1978).

6. The presence of clues or organizers before listening experiences consideraly influences the higher level listening skills and responses (Marten, 1978).

7. Although scores on listening tests and intelligence tests often are highly correlated, "there is enough variance in scores on the two kinds of tests not accounted for by the elements common to both to conclude that listening does depend on something besides intelligence" (Devine, 1978, p. 300).

8. There have been relatively few attempts to establish a research-based sequence of listening skills. "The few that are to be found are generally arbitrary selections. None seems to be based on actual research designed to discover which skill comes before another in terms of learning effectiveness or economy of teaching time" (Devine, 1978, p. 300).

9. A "cloze test" (in which words are deleted from sentences to determine vocabulary or syntactic skills) can be useful in measuring and improving listening skills (Marten, 1978).

10. Nonverbal cues contribute significantly to the meaning derived from social interactions (Wolvin and Coakley, 1979).

11.

12.

13.

## Research Findings: The Teaching of Writing

1. The study of grammar is an ineffective way to teach writing and takes time away from reading and writing (Petrosky, 1977).

2. Frequency of writing in and of itself is not associated with improvement of writing (Haynes, 1978).

3. There is a positive relationship between good writing and increased reading experiences (Blount, 1973).

4. Beneficial results accrue from the use of such prewriting procedures as thinking, talking, working in groups, role playing, interviews, debates, and problem solving (Haynes, 1978).

5. "Teachers should give greater emphasis to the guiding of careful development of a limited number of papers, with attention given to direct methods of instruction and to the solving of communication problems before and during the writing process, rather than on the hurried production of a great number of papers" (Haynes, 1978, p. 87).

6. There is some evidence that sentence-combining practice, without instruction in formal grammar, is an aid to syntactic fluency (Haynes, 1978).

7. While there seems to be no evidence to support one revision process over another, there is substantial evidence that the revision process itself is critical in improving writing (Bamberg, 1978).

8. The kind or intensity of teacher evaluation of composition is unrelated to the improvement in writing skill (Bamberg, 1978).

9. Written language is closely related to oral language. Teaching should emphasize and exploit the close connection between written and oral language (Lundsteen, 1976).

10. The quality of students' writing is unaffected by positive or negative criticism, but positive comments are more effective than negative ones in promoting positive attitudes toward writing (Van De Weghe, 1978).

11. Peer evaluation and editing are effective in improving writing skills (Van De Weghe, 1978).

12.

13.

14.

## Research Findings: Improving Reading Ability

1. A review of the research on the psycholinguistic aspects of reading suggests that the skilled, fluent reader uses the following strategies in reading: discovers distinctive features in letters, words, meanings; takes chances and risks errors in order to learn about the printed text and predict meaning; reads to identify meaning rather than words; guesses the meaning of unfamiliar words from context or skips them; takes an active role, bringing previous knowledge to bear on the text; reads as though he or she expects the text to make sense; makes use of redundancies to reduce uncertainty about meaning (Cooper and Petrosky, 1976).

2. "We do not know whether skilled reading is a holistic process or a set of interrelated subprocesses; researchers have not yet resolved this problem. . . . Based on our analysis of reading theory and research, we recommend for teaching purposes that reading be viewed as a set of subskills that can be taught and integrated" (Weaver and Shonkoff, 1978).

3. Reading comprehension seems to depend upon a number of component skills—word recognition, vocabulary knowledge, prior experience, and organization skills. The evidence seems to suggest that teachers should teach these skills concurrently, not sequentially (Weaver and Shonkoff, 1978).

4. Vocabulary-concept knowledge plays a major role in reading comprehension and is one area that seems slighted in most school programs; it is also an area where direct instruction would seem most helpful for economically disadvantaged students (Becker, 1977).

5. A number of investigations provide support for direct instruction in specific reading skills as they relate to the content areas; reading seems not to be a generalized skill but instead involves the ability to interpret a particular area of experience (Karlin, 1969).

6. Reading instruction in the secondary school seems in general to have a positive effect (Early, 1969).

7. The reading ability of gifted students varies; instruction to help them overcome specific deficiences will be beneficial (Karlin, 1969).

8. Perhaps as many as one-fourth of the students lack the skills they need to read the assigned books with the comprehension expected of them (Karlin, 1969).

9. There is some evidence that scores on reading comprehension achievement tests can be improved by preparing students for the test situation; exercises that reproduce the format, instructions, and time limits of such tests should reduce test anxiety and lead to improved performance (Weaver and Shonkoff, 1978).

10. Pre-questions before a test seem to increase the likelihood of students learning the specific information related to those questions; post-questions are preferable if students are to learn the general content (Weaver and Shonkoff, 1978).

11. It seems likely that speaking standard black English does not interfere with learning to read; teacher attitudes and expectations for students who speak black dialect may be a greater source of interference than the dialect itself (Weaver and Shonkoff, 1978).

12. "All methods of reading instruction instruct some children . . . well and do not succeed with some small proportion of others. . . . The national reading problem is not that massive numbers of students cannot read in the sense of not knowing grapheme-phoneme correspondences but that many persons do not wish to read for pleasure or information and do not comprehend either written or oral messages well. In effect, the national reading problem might just as easily be called the national thinking or comprehension problem, and the schools are only minutely responsible for the fact that massive numbers of our citizens are . . . not inclined to develop or maintain reading and comprehension skills necessary for their own self-selected goals . . ." (Diederich, 1973, p. 5).

13. The process of deriving meaning from sentences and paragraphs demands that readers process words without conscious

attention. If readers are forced to ponder over many words, they will be unable to comprehend what they are reading. This does not mean that every word readers encounter must be thoroughly familiar to them. But it does mean that preteaching difficult vocabulary can facilitate the reading process as students read a selection (Graves, Palmer, and Furniss, 1976).

14. Individualized reading programs facilitate reading achievement to the same extent as does a basal reading program, and often increase reading achievement; they have been used successfully at all grade levels (Thompson, 1975).

15.

16.

17.

## Research Findings: Facilitating the Response to Literature

1. Extensive reading of literature results in the reading of more books, in the development of more favorable attitudes toward books, and in continued growth of reading skills (Squire, 1969).
2. The student's "identity" may be the most important determinant of differences in the fictional experience; readers re-create what the writer has written in terms of their own

identity theme. Teachers need to appreciate the complex contribution of the student's past experience, fantasies, feelings, and identity needs (Beach and Cooper, 1974).

3. Response to literature is complex, influenced by factors such as personality, cognitive abilities, expectations, culture, reading ability, and schooling (Petrosky, 1977).

4. It seems reasonably safe to conclude that response to literature is developmental and that students will exhibit certain characteristics at certain stages of development (Petrosky, 1977).

5. Students can and do react to teacher question patterns and can be taught a variety of ways to develop breadth and depth in their responses (Petrosky, 1977).

6. Some research suggests that students at the junior high level are cognitively incapable of inferring symbols or themes, or they are too egocentric to assume the perspective of a character of a narrative (Beach and Cooper, 1974).

7. Problems in reading and understanding literature can be generalized as follows: insufficient information; failure to understand (diction, syntax, imagery and metaphor, inference about parts or whole, inference about characters, inference about tone or mood, inference about structure); psychological problems (aesthetic distance, preconceptions, tendency to invent or desire for happy ending, dominance of rhythm, feelings, lack of attention) (Purves and Beach, 1972).

8. The following factors of taste have been isolated: general liking, formal factors, content factors, personal factors, miscellaneous. The general factor is the most important in most judgments; the next most important factor seems to deal with the opposition of form and content or the personal appeal (Purves and Beach, 1972).

9. Inexperienced readers reject what they do not understand (Purves and Beach, 1972).

10. Nonprofessional responses to literature seem to fall into five general groupings: the personal statement (personal responses that refer to oneself and one's associations, and those that refer to one's feelings about the work and one's relation to it), descriptive responses, interpretative responses, evaluative

responses, and miscellaneous responses (Purves and Beach, 1972).

11. The dominant response of young readers deals with the content of the work, not its form, and with the work's relation to the reader and the reader's world, rather than with objective or aesthetic qualities of the work (Purves and Beach, 1972).

12. The subject matter of a work is interesting if it is related to the personal experience of the reader; people tend to become more involved in that which is related to them and tend to seek the work with which they can identify (Purves and Beach, 1972).

13. Instruction in literature affects taste and style of response (Purves and Beach, 1972).

14. "If one is looking for specific answers, directive teaching toward those answers will be successful; if one is looking for divergence, nondirective teaching will be successful" (Purves and Beach, 1972, p. 152).

15. The teacher and the kind of teacher intervention seem to have more effect on student response than particular types of curricular structure or sequence (Purves and Beach, 1972).

16.

17.

18.

## Research Findings: The Teaching of Spelling

1. Correct spelling can be predicted for a phoneme sound approximately 90 percent of the time when position, stress, and internal constraints are considered (Geedy, 1975).

2. There is as yet no field-tested substitute for direct instruction on the basic core of high-frequency words needed by children and adults in their writing (Horn, 1969).

3. Spelling ability and reading ability are highly correlated (Horn, 1969).

4. It is more efficient to study words from lists, rather than from context; words are learned more quickly, are more easily remembered, and are more readily transferred to a new context (Geedy, 1975).

5. The test-study-test method is more effective than the study-test method (Allred, 1977).

6. The self-corrected test seems to be a useful and an effective way to teach spelling (Allred, 1977).

7. The following eight-step method seems to be supported by much expert testimony and research: pronounce the word carefully, look carefully at each part, say the letters in sequence, try to recall how the word looks and spell the word to yourself, check your spelling, write the word, check the spelling, repeat if necessary (Allred, 1977).

8. Only a few rules should be taught—those with few or no exceptions. In teaching spelling rules the following practices should be observed: teach one rule at a time; teach the rule inductively; teach it when needed; stress the application of the rule; teach the exceptions to the rule; review the rule frequently (Allred, 1977).

9. Auditory discrimination and visual memory are key factors in good spelling (Allred, 1977).

10. Calling attention to the "hard spots" in a word seems to be a waste of time (Sherwin, 1969).

11. There seems to be no advantage in presenting words in a syllabified form (Horn, 1969).

12. Kinesthetic techniques, such as tracing, have proven useful with poor spellers and slow learners (Horn, 1969).

13.




14.




15.




## Research Findings: The Teaching of Grammar

1. Teachers should understand the distinctions among three commonly confused terms: *linguistics* is the scientific study of language; it includes *grammar*, the principles of word and sentence formation, and *usage*, the changing fashions of so-called correctness within regional and social dialects (Fraser and Hodson, 1978).

2. "Apart from scant evidence for the existence of some kind of distinction between a deep structure and a surface structure, there is no coherent body of experimental work to suggest that linguistic theory has contributed to either psychological or educational research in any direct way" (Ortony, 1975, p. 500).

3. The study of traditional grammar does not help a student write better and, in fact, may hinder development as a writer (Abrahamson, 1977).

4. Diagraming does not work well enough to justify all the time and bother; it also seems to perpetuate a distorted and

incomplete picture of English structure because of its depend-
ence upon a Latinate grammar (Sherwin, 1969).

5. Instruction in mechanics is most effective in the rewriting
   stage, in response to an individual's need; previous teaching
   of grammatical terminology is unnecessary (Weaver, 1979).

6. There is some tentative evidence that writing activities
   designed to enhance syntactic skills will lead to improved
   reading comprehension (Stotsky, 1975).

7.

8.

9.

# 11 Developing the English Notebook

You now have in hand the final version of the content planning matrix. It shows for only the mastery curriculum what general concepts and skills are taught, level by level. It has been evaluated carefully from several perspectives and represents the best judgment of classroom teachers, instructional leaders, and consultants. Now the challenge is to use the content matrix as a planning device for producing usable curricular materials that will meet the criteria suggested in Chapter 1:

1. The format in which the curriculum guide is delivered to the teachers should be flexible, able to accommodate a variety of teaching styles, and not require radical changes in teaching style.
2. The format should be usable and open; it should be one that teachers will use and add to.
3. The format should be one that can readily accommodate computers and video devices.

Here is an outline of the general nature of the proposed format, followed by details on how it might be produced.

The basic format is a large loose-leaf notebook for each teacher. At the outset, all notebooks contain only two common parts: (1) a copy of the content planning matrix for all grade levels; and (2) a summary of departmental policies and practices on grading, book distribution, cumulative records, and so on.

All other parts described below will vary in content, depending on which grade level the notebook is intended for.

Each notebook is divided into the several areas of the curriculum used in the mapping and matrix projects. A notebook organized according to the plan given in the example would therefore have eight major sections: reading and study skills, literature and media, composition, grammar and language, word study and vocabulary, speaking and listening, critical and creative thinking, and spelling, punctuation, and usage.

When the notebooks are first distributed, each major section includes three kinds of items. First each section contains a summary of the research relating to that area or aspect of English. Thus, the composition section begins with a summary of the research on composition. The important research for each area of English is summarized in Chapter 10 in a form convenient for photocopying. (To save time, simply make a photocopy of the appropriate pages from this work and insert them in the notebooks.) Second, each section includes the course objectives for that grade only, grouped according to the component strand, for each general skill or concept. (An explanation of how to write these objectives is given below.) Thus, the eighth grade teacher would receive the course objectives for only grade eight. Third, each section includes a brief list of *available* materials relating to that section.

All the notebook contains, then, is the content planning matrix for all grades; a summary of departmental policies; summaries of the research for the various aspects of English; lists of course objectives; and brief lists of materials. It does not contain a statement of philosophy or a rationale. It does not contain suggestions about how to teach. It does not include examinations or suggestions about testing. It does not include detailed units of study. It is lean, thin, bare-boned. And I think the format conveys an important message to the teachers: This is the content you are expected to teach—and you are free to teach it as you wish.

## Adding Items of Personal Interest

The hope is that teachers will add to their notebooks as they see fit. They might add items such as these: journal articles relating to one or another of the areas; classroom learning exercises; copies of tests; units they and their colleagues have written; examples of student work. And they would be encouraged to update the research review section, adding recent findings of importance.

Besides inviting teacher contributions and additions, the notebook facilitates future departmental modifications and additions. Materials to be deleted are simply torn out; new concepts and objectives are added where they belong. If, later on, the department decides to write mastery units or learning packages, these can also be added.

What disadvantages does such a format have? There are two. New teachers especially may miss the organized units of study typically found in most guides; but they would profit more from having an experienced colleague help them develop their own units from the concepts and objectives. And loose-leaf pages have a way of falling out and getting lost; but that's a small price to pay for the flexibility and open-endedness of the format.

The notebooks should be easy to produce and assemble. The instructional leader is responsible for providing only the content planning matrix, statement of department policies, and lists of available materials. The writing teams produce the course objectives, and here is a suggestion for the best way to accomplish this.

For purposes of illustration, suppose that you have been given the task of writing the course objectives for grade eight. You decide to begin with the area of composition. Since you feel confident of your knowledge of expository writing, you choose that strand for writing the first set of objectives. Note that the general skill to be mastered is writing an expository essay that "explains a process." You also observe that the seventh grade unit is designated as "giving directions." You can assume, therefore, that some basic expository skills will be taught in seventh grade. (After all objectives have been developed, you will, of course, check to ensure that there is smooth progression from grade to grade and that there are no significant gaps.) You reflect about your knowledge of typical eighth graders and how much they know in general about writing. What you are doing in this mental review is establishing in your mind a tentative list of the cognitive entry characteristics—the basic skills that will be needed to begin the unit but will not be taught in the unit itself. These cognitive entry characteristics need not be identified at this stage as part of the unit, but they are useful if you decide later on to use a mastery learning approach (see Chapter 15).

You now turn your attention to the eighth grade unit. You make some tentative decisions about it, based upon your previous analyses: It will emphasize a short essay explaining something the eighth grader knows from direct experience, written for a specific audience. Now, to determine the essential objectives, you perform a task analysis of writing that essay. You think about the essential characteristics of an excellent student essay of the sort you have in mind. You outline the specific skills that should be mastered in order to write that essay. You review your list, trying to pare it down to the essentials. Then you write the final list, using a "Mastery Objectives" form like the one shown in Figure 9.

In general the process will be the same with all units. You determine the cognitive entry characteristics by thinking generally about the nature of the unit, the maturity of the students, and the extent of their prior learning. You then do a task analysis of general skill or knowledge to be emphasized, deciding what skills and knowledge are essential in achieving the goal you have specified. You write up that list of knowledges and skills as a set of mastery objectives, using a form like the one in Figure 9.

## Listing the Objectives

Note some special points about the mastery objectives form. First, the general skill or concept is identified in the manner in which it was presented in the matrix. Then the writer has restated it in greater detail. Next, the specific objectives are listed in logical sequence. Each objective begins with a verb, but in my opinion there is no need to use precise behavioral language or to state a criterion level of performance. The goal here is to help the teacher understand what skills to stress, not to provide a set of specifications for a test. The comments at the bottom call attention to special features of that set of objectives.

Although some may feel uneasy about any system that smacks of computers and management, it is suggested that a simple numbering system be used to facilitate computer management and video retrieval. The first digits (under "Course Objectives") are the grade or level; in the example, 08. The second digit is the area of the curriculum, composition, here assigned the number 2. The next two digits identify the component; in this case, expository writing is designated as component 04. The last two digits number the specific objectives.

When the course objective sheets have been written, they should be reviewed by the instructional leader and the task force, with these criteria in mind:

1. Is the general concept or skill restated accurately and expanded appropriately?

2. Are the related objectives restated at an appropriate level of specificity?

3. Do the specific objectives cover all the important skills or subconcepts?

4. Does the list include only essential objectives?

As the teachers use the mastery objectives forms, they will, of course, be encouraged to evaluate them and forward their criticisms to you. When you receive such evaluations, you can either decide to issue revised forms at once or wait until some later date when you can thoroughly revise the whole notebook.

I believe that the format described above meets the criteria stated at the opening of this chapter. The loose-leaf notebook is flexible; it leaves to the teacher important decisions about teaching methods and organizational strategies. It is in a form which teachers can easily use and can adapt to their own needs by contributing their own ideas—and it readily accommodates computer and video retrieval systems. Finally, as explained in later chapters, the form can be used in a variety of curricular and instructional approaches.

# 12 Using Separate Objectives in Integrated Units

The English notebook with its content planning matrix and lists of related mastery objectives can be the end point of the curriculum process—or it can be the foundation of future developmental work. Although the objectives have been grouped by area of the discipline, they can be flexibly used as the basis for writing integrated language arts units, interdisciplinary humanities courses, or thematic electives. This chapter will explain their use in developing integrated language arts units and succeeding chapters will deal with the other two issues.

At the outset, however, some definitions are needed. For the sake of clarity, the following three definitions are stipulated for the types of units and courses which can be developed.

A *focused unit* is a curriculum unit in which all concepts, skills, and objectives relate to a single area of a given discipline. The organizing theme of such a unit is the general concept or skill directly related to that area or component. Thus, a focused unit of study in English would be one in which all the objectives related, for example, to the writing of an expository essay. The organizing theme would be "writing the expository essay."

An *integrated unit* is a curriculum unit in which the concepts, skills, and objectives are drawn from two or more areas of a single discipline. The organizing theme of such a unit would be some general idea (such as "The Colonial Spirit") which links the several classes of concepts, skills, and objectives from the areas of reading, writing, speaking, and grammar.

An *interdisciplinary unit* or *course* is one in which the concepts, skills, and objectives are drawn from two or more disciplines. The organizing theme of the unit is a general idea which relates those disciplines. Thus, an interdisciplinary unit of study might have "Conflict and Violence" as its theme, including concepts, skills, and objectives from English, social studies, art, and science.

Before examining a process for writing integrated units, it might be useful to review the arguments for such units. Most leaders in the field of English curriculum strongly recommend such units, basing their argument on the integrated nature of language. Moffett and Wagner (1976, p. 42) state the case most persuasively:

> The environment for language learning must preserve the truth about language: as the main ingredient in our symbolic life it not only operates within every aspect of our lives but part of its very function is to integrate the diversity of experience into a harmonious whole.

Along with most other curriculum writers, they fulminate against what they call "the particle approach," the teaching of "isolated parts." Spann and Culp (1977), editors of a recent collection of thematic or integrated units, are even more enthusiastic about integrated units. In their introductory comments (p. *iii*) they make these observations:

> The current nationwide emphasis on basic skills has not changed our point of view. The units in this first supplement . . . have been selected . . . because they involve students actively in reading, writing, listening, and speaking for a purpose—that purpose being to explore and communicate with others on issues of vital interest to all. In our view nothing could be more basic. In our dedication to the humanistic, thematic approach to the teaching of English, we have not ignored other approaches. We have studied and discussed the advantages and disadvantages of each prescribed method, but have consistently found that a concern with values is the most successful way of stimulating students to reflect on, probe into, and act upon problems directly affecting their own lives.

Yet while there is an abundance of exhortation about the advantages of integrated units, there is a paucity of research. And the available research does not support the claims of those advocating the integrated study of English. Boehnlein and Ritty (1977, p. 375) summarize their careful review of all such research with this somewhat discouraging conclusion:

> While it is easy to find journal articles and language arts methods textbooks advocating an integrated or correlated approach to teaching, there appears to be no empirical research to support this advocacy; a disturbing finding.

A somewhat similar conclusion is reached by Walker and Schaffarzick (1974, p. 97) in their review of the research on so-called innovative curricula:

> . . . different curricula produce different patterns of achievement, not necessarily greater overall achievement. What these studies show apparently, is *not* that the new curricula are uniformly superior to the old ones, though this may be true, but rather that

> *different curricula are associated with different patterns of achievement.* Furthermore, these different patterns of achievement seem generally to follow patterns apparent in the curricula. [Italics in original.]

We might restate Walker and Schaffarzick's conclusion in this way: If we were to compare an integrated unit on "Choosing a Career" (which taught the writing of the expository essay as an incidental topic) with a focused unit on "Writing the Expository Essay" (which asked the student to write about careers), we would find that the unit on career choice did a better job of teaching career-selection skills, and the unit on the expository essay achieved better results in teaching the expository essay.

It seems reasonable to conclude that an English curriculum that includes some focused units and some integrated units would reap the advantages of both approaches. But such a decision is best left to grade-level teams or individual teachers who can consider such factors as the age of their students, the level of student motivation, the students' ability, the availability of materials, and their own predilections. If the team decides to use integrated units, then the issue of the relationship between integrated units and mastery content must be addressed.

There are essentially three ways of viewing this relationship.

1. Integrated thematic units will constitute the entire curriculum. They will be planned in a way that stresses the theme and makes extensive provisions for reading, writing, speaking, and listening. No special planning for including mastery concepts and skills is considered necessary.

2. Integrated thematic units will be included only to increase motivation and provide for a change of pace. Only a few integrated units will be taught. Since they will not make specific provision for mastery content, there is no need for systematic planning. All mastery content will be taught in focused units.

3. Both focused and integrated units will be taught, with some of the mastery concepts and skills to be taught in integrated units.

If this last choice is made, then the leader and the team need to use a systematic method of deciding on the allocation of mastery content to focused and integrated units. I would like to suggest one such method, before proceeding to some suggestions for the planning of integrated units.

The first concern is to allocate mastery skills and concepts to focused or integrated units in a manner that eliminates needless repetition and unintentional omission. The initial step is to decide on the number and organizing themes of the integrated units. These organizing themes can be of several sorts:

Life skills: Choosing a Career; Solving School and Community Problems

Literary genres: The Comic Spirit; Fantastic Worlds

Places: The Voice of the South; New York, New York

Eras and ages: The Thirties; the Medieval Mind

Problems and issues: Environmental Crisis; Divorce and Separation

Ethnic groups: The Black Experience; Chicano Voices

Sex: Machismo; Women in Contemporary Fiction

Adolescent interests: The Spirit of Sports; the Roots of American Music

Artistic works: The Book of Job; Greek and Roman Myths

Real and imaginary people: The Devil in Literature; The World of Mark Twain

"Big ideas": Love Is a Many-Splendored Thing; The Faces of Peace

A theme for an integrated unit should meet several obvious criteria. First, it should reflect the interests of the teaching team, since teacher enthusiasm and competence are important elements in successful units. Second, it should appeal to students and respond to their interests. Third, the theme should be one that easily permits the integration of content from several areas of English and one for which good materials are readily available. Next, it should not repeat a theme taught in a previous year. Even if the content is different, students are likely to complain, "We did 'Good and Evil' last year." Finally, there should be some variety in the kinds of themes selected for a given year. If all themes deal with "eras and ages," for example, the result will be a slighting of other important concerns.

## Mechanics of the Unit Planning Chart

Once the themes or titles of units have been tentatively selected, they should be listed on a chart similar to the "Unit Planning Chart" shown in Figure 10. The category "focused unit" and the titles of all the integrated units should be listed across the top, and the mastery skills and concepts identified in the content planning matrix for that grade level should be listed down the left side of the chart.

The instructional leader and the team should then identify those concepts and skills that they think should be taught in separate focused units, and mark them with an *X* under the column headed "focused unit." These principles should be kept in mind in making this decision:

1. Any skill which is a state-or-locally-mandated competency is probably best taught as a separate focused unit. So if tenth grade students face a test covering the interpretation of non-verbal symbols, they will be helped most with a unit focusing on that skill.

2. Any skill or concept which is complex and difficult probably is best mastered in a focused unit. Trying to integrate the teaching of the term paper into a unit on "the comic spirit," for example, either slights the term paper or distorts the unit.

3. Any skill or concept which is not readily integrated with other content is probably best taught as a focused unit. If it is considered important for students to be able to identify the parts of speech, then these concepts are probably best taught in a focused unit, since such content does not lend itself readily to integration.

With the focused units identified, the leader and the team should then decide where each mastery concept or skill not allocated to a focused unit can best be integrated. When they have made this decision, they should indicate with an *X*, the mastery concepts and skills under the title of the unit in which it will receive primary emphasis.

Such a process ensures that each mastery skill or concept will either be taught separately in a focused unit or emphasized in an integrated unit. The group may also wish to note which mastery skills and concepts may receive incidental treatment, making an appropriate notation on the chart. Figure 10 shows how a tenth grade team might handle the mastery skills and concepts for composition.

The leader and the team are now ready for the specific planning of integrated units. How can integrated units best be planned? There are, of course, many excellent guides available which explain how to write standard curriculum units. I would like to describe my own approach to integration, which I think offers some special advantages, by showing how a sample unit on "Divorce and Separation" might be planned. (I would like to acknowledge my indebtedness to Eugene Bledsoe for suggestions about content and objectives drawn from his unit on "Teaching About Divorce," reprinted in Spann and Culp, 1977.)

Suppose that a teaching team had to write an integrated unit on "Divorce and Separation" for tenth grade students—and they want the unit to include appropriate mastery content. How do they proceed? They begin by deciding on the length of the unit—how much time it should take. This depends, of course, on the motivation and interest of students, the total amount of time available for the course, the time requirements of other units, and the complexity of the unit under consideration. Let's assume in this instance that three weeks (fifteen lessons) are allocated.

The next step is to consider four general kinds of outcomes: thematic understandings, common readings, mastery concepts and skills, and organic learnings. Each is briefly explained as follows:

1. Thematic understandings are the theme-related knowledge, insights, and ideas which the teacher plans to stress through the unit.

2. Common readings are the books, articles, plays, and poems which all students will be expected to read. If longer films or videotapes are to be seen by the class, these also should be included here. (Note that the term *reading* is used to include the study of both print and visual works.)

3. Integrated mastery concepts and skills are taken from the unit planning chart (Figure 10) or from an analysis of what mastery content should be included.

4. Organic learnings, as explained in Chapter 4, are the important basic learnings which are not structured into separate units but are nurtured organically by the teacher at every appropriate juncture. As noted before, the author's preference is for all affective outcomes to be included in the organic component.

The decisions about the kinds of outcomes expected from the unit should be recorded down the left-hand side of a "Unit Outcomes" chart (Figure 11). Columns for the lessons are listed across the top.

How are such decisions made? The answer will vary, of course, with the planner. Perhaps these general suggestions will be of help: First, begin by thinking about the thematic outcomes. Based upon your analysis of the unit theme, what important general understandings and insights do you hope to develop? One admonition here is not to be too ambitious. I have seen several integrated units fail because they tried to achieve too many lofty aims. A sample list of thematic understandings for this particular unit is offered in Figure 11.

Next, survey the resources that are available. By reviewing district reading lists, thematically organized bibliographies, anthologies, and your own collection of materials, choose readings that relate to the theme. Besides having thematic relevance, the readings should meet these other criteria:

1. They are accessible and interesting to teenage readers.
2. They are sufficiently challenging to warrant class study and discussion.
3. They are not likely to offend students and their parents.
4. They represent a diversity of types, periods, and perspectives.

The decisions about the thematic understandings and the common readings are of course interrelated. Some planners start with themes and choose works, others begin with important works and elicit relevant themes, and still others weigh both considerations in an interactive fashion.

The list of mastery concepts and skills is drawn from the previous analysis reflected in Figure 11. And the decision about which organic learnings should be included derives primarily from an analysis of the learner's needs as they relate to this specific thematic unit.

## Integration of Outcomes

With these four kinds of outcomes listed on the chart, the next step is making an interrelated decision about articulation and sequencing: Which outcomes can be most readily integrated and in which sequence should they be taught? It is best to sense the general rhythm of the unit first. I think about the ideas and the works and the teenagers I know, to get a general sense of how the work should flow. In this particular unit, the first week starts with the present, with some close reading and discussion of controversial articles; then the second week moves back a little in time and includes a slower, more reflective analysis of a major play; and the third week ends with some active learning, focusing on feelings and attitudes. These general impressions are then translated into tentative decisions about the sequencing of the common readings.

At the same time, some related decisions are made about how those common readings are linked to the thematic understandings, the mastery skills, and the organic learnings. The relationship of the mastery skills to the common readings is given special consideration, for the skills must be taught effectively and should seem to relate naturally to the whole unit. In this particular unit, two of the skills relate directly to the readings: The close reading of nonfiction can be easily taught when the articles are read, and the analysis of the literary symbol is naturally linked to the study of the longer play. Paragraph skills are then taught as part of an assigned theme in which the students are expected to respond to the articles they have read during the first week.

These tentative decisions are recorded on the chart, using the letter $E$ to indicate when the skills and concepts will be emphasized and the letter $R$ when reviewed. A final review is made of both the interrelationships of concepts and content and the distribution of the content over the three-week span. The final form of the chart is then used as a map for planning and writing the other materials that will make up the unit distributed to those who will teach it. My preference is for a compact unit which includes only such essential materials as: (1) one-page overview of the unit, (2) the Unit Outcomes chart, (3) copies of articles and shorter works, (4) study guides for the longer literary works, (5) objectives for the mastery content, (6) suggestions for integrating organic learnings, and (7) lists of related—and available—materials. This collection of materials can then be added to the English notebook.

There are several points to emphasize here about this process and product. Observe that it is a "top-down" planning process which begins with a decision about the works to be taught and the general outcomes to be achieved. It does not begin with long lists of specific objectives. Note as well, in this context, that specific objectives are provided only for the mastery content. Finally, only materials that will help teachers do their own, more detailed planning are included in the unit. There is no attempt to describe each lesson in detail or to specify teaching methods.

The process may perhaps seem a bit complicated, but it actually is a simple one which can be used to develop interesting integrated units that provide effectively for mastery.

# 13 Building English Mastery into Interdisciplinary Courses

There are several signs that interdisciplinary humanities courses, which flourished in the schools in the early 1960s, are once again attracting the attention of curriculum specialists and teachers. For example, the November 1978 issue of the journal *Educational Leadership*, which was devoted to the theme "The Patchwork Curriculum," included several articles attacking "curricular fragmentation" and advocating "curricular integration." And, as noted previously, the *English Journal* of February 1980 was devoted to discussions of humanities courses. So it seems to be an appropriate time to consider how to design such courses in a way that does not neglect the mastery components of English.

First, a definition is in order because the term *humanities* has been used in so many ways. In some circles it seems only to be a vague honorific, foolishly equated with attempts to make courses more relevant for and interesting to students. In other usage it unfortunately is restricted to interdisciplinary offerings that usually draw content from the areas of literature and history. My preference is to use a more traditional definition:

> The humanities are those courses of study in school and college which singly or in combination draw most of their content from the disciplines of literature, history, religion, philosophy, language, art (academic, not studio, courses), and music (academic, not performing, courses).

In designing such courses the teacher or curriculum specialist has a variety of options available. I would like to use the following adjectives to label these options: *separate, articulated, correlated, interdisciplinary, isolated.*

*Separate* courses are the traditional means by which humanities offerings have been developed. (And here, of course, "traditional" is not intended as a pejorative.) Each teacher or department develops separate courses in a particular field. The only concern is to make an individual course as strong as possible. The advantage of the separate course is that it enables the course developer to focus on the unique characteristics and structures of a particular discipline, without being distracted by questions of interdisciplinary relationships. Critics of the separate course approach allege that the resulting program of studies makes it difficult for the student to see connections and relationships among the disciplines. And note here, of course, that separate courses can be developed around focused or integrated units of study, as explained in the previous chapter.

*Articulated* courses are separate courses that have been loosely linked or articulated. While there is no attempt to develop parallel course offerings as in the options described below, there is a concern for ensuring that the separate courses do not contradict each other, repeat each other, or omit important concepts or skills. The advantage of the articulated approach, according to its advocates, is that it retains the integrity of each discipline while avoiding the dangers of fragmentation and lack of coordination.

The following process is recommended for those who are interested in articulating humanities offerings:

1. Develop what might be termed an "articulation matrix." Begin by listing down the left all the skills and concepts that might be involved in the articulation process. Do not list content that obviously falls within the purview of a given discipline. The concern, instead, is to list that content and those skills that are more likely to be omitted or duplicated. Across the top of the matrix list all the specific courses involved in the articulation process. The matrix will look something like this:

### Articulation Matrix

| Content/Course | English 1 | English 2 | English 3 | U.S. History | Western Civilization | World Cultures |
|---|---|---|---|---|---|---|
| Research paper | | | | | | |
| Mass media | | | | | | |
| Current affairs | | | | | | |
| Critical reading | | | | | | |
| Critical thinking | | | | | | |
| Creative thinking | | | | | | |

2. Circulate the matrix to all teachers involved. Ask them to indicate by means of a simple code how much attention the listed items receive in the courses they teach (M = much; S = some; L = little or none).

3. Collate the results on a master chart.

4. Hold a series of meetings of all those involved, to review the results and to develop plans for improving articulation. Where omissions have been detected, determine where that skill should be taught—unless it appears that the omission is an unimportant one. Where repetitions have been noted, decide where the skill should receive primary attention and where it may simply need to be reinforced.

*Correlated* courses are separate courses that have been specifically designed to deal with the same period of time at a similar point in the year's schedule. Thus, while students are studying the Revolution in the U.S. History course, they are also studying the literature of the Revolution in the English course. The advantages of correlation are obvious. The student probably achieves a greater depth of understanding of a given period of history by examining that period from the perspectives of at least two different disciplines. The separate disciplines are thus perceived as reinforcing each other. The correlated approach also facilitates interdepartmental planning and communication.

The disadvantages should be weighed as well. First, in most such attempts the history course plays the dominant role: The English course is planned to accommodate the chronology of the history course. Second, each course involved must make some compromises that result in unwise allocations of time. So the English teacher spends too much time on unimportant diarists of the Colonial period to keep the history teacher happy, or the history teacher allocates too much time to the post–Civil War period just to please the English teacher.

One solution that eliminates these drawbacks is to develop a plan for modified correlation. Each department involved draws up its own outline for the year, indicating approximate time allocations for the major units of study. The two departments meet together to review the individual proposals and to decide where some reasonable compromises can be made. Thus, if each department has planned fifteen two-week units for the year, they might decide that only six of those units can be effectively correlated. The correlation is thus limited to those units of study where some depth of treatment seems warranted by all the disciplines involved.

*Interdisciplinary* courses are those in which two or more disciplines have been fused into a single course. An American Studies course, for example, would be a single course which would integrate content from American history, English, art, music, religion, and philosophy in a study of the American experience. The distinctions between the disciplines are usually minimized; the emphasis is on the culture or the area, not a particular discipline.

Interdisciplinary courses are usually taught by an interdisciplinary team using a longer block of time, but they need not be linked with team teaching. A carefully developed interdisciplinary course could be taught by one well-prepared teacher.

Interdisciplinary courses obviously result in a program of studies that appears to be more cohesive. The way in which the course is planned seems to ensure that the student will examine major problems and movements in a coherent fashion, not from isolated perspectives. Such courses also probably require a greater degree of interdepartmental cooperation and communication, and such an end ordinarily seems desirable. The disadvantages are linked to the advantages. There are those who feel that interdisciplinary courses slight the skills and concepts unique to a given discipline, and some teachers involved with such courses complain about the inordinate amount of time required for team planning and team teaching.

*Isolated* courses, as the term is used here, are humanities courses offered independently of the rest of the curriculum, usually as an elective. Thus, a student might be taking a series of separate courses in English, history, and art but would also have the opportunity of enrolling in a separate course called Humanities. In a sense, then, the isolated humanities course is an interdisciplinary course offered in addition to (instead of in place of) the regular course offerings. The isolated courses usually are planned to deal with content not covered in the standard courses—knowledge that falls between or transcends the disciplines.

Their main advantage is that they are freed from the constraints of the disciplines. Course planners are able to focus on important problems and issues without worrying about the skills and structures of a given discipline. Thus the isolated courses are more likely to draw content from the natural sciences and the social sciences as well as from the humanities. The main problem with isolated courses is that they require their own special resources—time, teachers, texts—and such resources are scarce. Critics also complain that many isolated courses lack intellectual rigor, although this obviously need not be the case.

Those who develop interdisciplinary or isolated courses can fashion them around a large number of what I call "organizing centers." The organizing center of a course is the intellectual basis for structuring the course. As it is beyond the scope of this work to discuss in full all the possible organizing centers, here is a list of several of them, and a few examples for each:

1. Area studies. American Studies, The Far East.
2. Ethnic and women's studies. The Black Experience, The American Woman.
3. Culture epochs. The Renaissance, Classical Greece.
4. Great works. The Great Books.
5. Aesthetic structures. Symbolism—Visual and Verbal.
6. Career studies. Humanities and Law Enforcement.
7. Themes and ideas. Conflict and Violence, Moral Dilemmas in Contemporary America.

Obviously a given course could be built around one or several organizing structures.

Note here a distinction between what I call "organizing centers" and "instructional systems," since the two are often confused. As explained above, the organizing center is so called to identify the kind of abstraction that governs how content is selected and organized. An instructional system, on the other hand, is a set of arrangements by which learning is facilitated; it involves decisions about matters of staffing, group size, media, methodology, space, and teacher-learner interaction.

Here are some of the instructional systems typically used in interdisciplinary courses, since this work does not propose to examine them in detail:

1. Team teaching—groups of teachers planning collaboratively and sharing the teaching.
2. Flexible group size—large, small, laboratory group.
3. Flexible time arrangements—modular schedules, blocks of time.
4. Independent study—a variety of systems that facilitate self-instruction and inquiry.
5. Resource rooms—special areas equipped with media and materials for the study of humanities.

It is evident that the person designing humanities offerings faces a confusing array of choices. Is there any reliable research available to guide the decision-making process? Unfortunately, there is not much. This does not mean that the literature of the field is scant—in fact, there are hundreds of articles about humanities and interdisciplinary courses. Unfortunately, almost all of them are polemics ("let's end curricular fragmentation"), show-and-tell descriptions ("this is how I designed this marvelous course") or testimonials ("the students all said it was the best course they ever had").

The few valid research studies available do not demonstrate that any given design option is superior to any other. In fact, they suggest quite the opposite. Walker (1977, pp. 272–273) summarizes his results in this fashion:

> In those studies for which such a profile of results could be derived, the achievement test profiles seemed to parallel patterns of content inclusion and emphasis in the curricula being compared. . . . The well-designed studies succeeded at best in showing that when curricula have different effects, the differences are roughly what we would expect to find if we simply compared in a common-sense fashion their content and objectives. This confirmation that curricula were producing roughly the patterns of achievement their developers had intended could be seen as heartening.

To relate this general finding to the question at hand, one might conclude as follows: Courses designed to emphasize interdisciplinary relationships achieve this objective better than courses not so designed; courses designed to stress the conceptual structure of a given discipline achieve this objective better than courses not so designed.

There are, however, some common-sense insights derived from observation, practice, and reflection that might be useful:

1. Separate courses are probably easiest to design.
2. Courses that require team planning require more teacher time than do courses planned otherwise.
3. Some teachers work well in collaborative arrangements; others seem to be more effective when they are able to work alone.
4. New courses succeed when the teachers involved are strongly committed to them and when the administrators deliver the necessary support.
5. Students who are deficient in communication and computation skills seem to require specific instruction in those skills.
6. Students who must take competency tests, achievement tests, or advanced placement tests will do better on those tests when they have had sufficient opportunity to master the content typically included in such examinations.

In deciding which design options might best be used (and obviously it is both possible and probably desirable to include more than one in a multi-year program), I recommend that a planning team proceed as follows:

1. Identify the humanities goals or outcomes considered most important. An instrument which faculty can use to identify priority goals is shown in Figure 12. Teachers can use it, modify it, or develop their own.

2. Identify the constraints that affect planning—state requirements, school graduation requirements, other external limitations.

3. Evaluate the instructional context. Assess factors such as facilities, school schedule, community resources.

4. Analyze relevant information about the students for whom the program is being designed—general intelligence, reading ability, past achievement, career goals, preferred learning styles.

5. Assess faculty competence, preparation, and attitudes.

6. Develop several alternative design proposals.

7. Evaluate the proposals in terms of the goals previously set and the several assessments suggested above.

8. Check with the administrator to ensure that the design finally selected is acceptable and feasible.

These decisions can be systematized by recording them in a chart similar to the one shown in Figure 13. The entries in the chart represent recommendations for humanities offerings to a Catholic high school faculty with whom the author consulted as a member of the National Humanities Faculty. The faculty was interested in developing a comprehensive humanities program for their ablest students and seemed to find the recommendations useful in clarifying the several options available.

If it has been decided to develop interdisciplinary courses, some very careful planning is in order, to ensure that the units developed not only achieve the interdisciplinary outcomes but also make sufficient provision for the teaching of mastery content. One process which I believe will achieve both goals is outlined below. The process is more complex, obviously, than the one used for developing integrated courses because several disciplines are involved, but the basic strategy is the same.

First, the interdisciplinary teachers should decide on the organizing center for the course and then agree on the number and themes of the units to be developed. Assume, for example, that an interdisciplinary team of English, social studies, and art teachers has chosen "The Humanities in Contemporary American Life" as its organizing center. Through a series of team meetings, the team has decided to focus on twelve units of study: Violence in America, The Persistence of Virtue, American Heroes and Heroines, American Women, The American Family, Working in the United States, Love American Style, American Youth, Sports as Myth, Black Voices, The New Hispanics, Poverty and Affluence in America.

The next decision is to identify for each unit the major contribution to be made by the disciplines represented in the course. Here again the tentative team decisions should be recorded on a simple chart so that the team can see both interdisciplinary relationships and intradisciplinary developments over the span of a year. Figure 14 illustrates a team's decisions about the contribution of each discipline to the unit on "American Women."

Following this, teachers representing a given discipline should meet separately to make some tentative decisions as to where mastery content can best be taught, using the process explained in Chapter 12. As suggested there, they should decide for all mastery content whether that particular skill or concept can best be taught through a focused or an integrated approach. However, I recommend one minor distinction in the way in which this decision is perceived and recorded. Since the interdisciplinary course involves teachers from several disciplines and also probably involves a large block of time, separate focused units on English skills would seem inappropriate; all major units of study in an interdisciplinary course will probably be integrated thematic units. Therefore, the choice seems to be whether to teach mastery content here as focused lessons or integrated lessons. In teaching a focused mastery lesson on noun clauses, for example, the English teachers simply break the flow of the thematic unit and say, "Let's take a direct look at noun clauses today and maybe tomorrow. Then we'll get back to the theme of the unit." In teaching an integrated lesson, they say, "As you prepare to write your essay on the nature of contemporary heroes, we want to teach you some important skills in eliminating paragraph problems."

It is therefore recommended that they list on a chart, as in Figure 15, all titles of the integrated thematic units and the mastery concepts of skills, using the letters *FML* to indicate that a focused mastery lesson on a particular English skill will be taught in the time provided for that unit, and the letters *IML* to show that that mastery skill will be made an integral part of the thematic unit. The results of such individual planning by each discipline should then be reviewed by the entire team, to ensure that there is a relatively even distribution of mastery content throughout the course and that a particular unit is not overloaded with subject-centered mastery content.

The next step involves some careful planning of unit content, week by week. Here each discipline must determine for each unit how it will contribute to the important outcomes of the unit. At this point as well, the planning of interdisciplinary courses will follow the same general strategy as that used in developing integrated units, with some specific differences in the details. In planning for interdisciplinary outcomes, I recommend that these four kinds be identified:

1. Thematic understandings. As explained in Chapter 12, these are the central ideas or understandings that make up the intellectual content of that unit, the central thematic issues as they relate to particular disciplines.

2. Supporting learnings. This is a new class of outcomes. They are the related ideas or subordinate concepts undergirding the thematic understandings. Usually they are contributed by one of the disciplines not centrally involved with a given thematic understanding.

3. Integrated mastery outcomes. These are the mastery outcomes that will be integrated with theme-centered lessons.

4. Focused mastery outcomes. These are the mastery outcomes that will be treated in separate focused lessons.

Besides adding the class of so-called supporting learnings, this grouping of outcomes differs from that used in integrated units in three other ways. First, so-called common readings are not identified at this stage but can be added later; the category seems inappropriate for disciplines other than English. Second, the mastery outcomes have been differentiated as both integrated and focused outcomes, since these units will include both. Finally, to simplify the planning of interdisciplinary units, the category of organic learnings is dropped. These also can be added later if teachers prefer. The general point is that interdisciplinary planning is less detailed and subject-specific than integrated unit planning.

Figure 16 shows how a team of English, social studies, and art teachers might decide on their respective contributions to the thematic understandings and supporting learning of a three-week "American Women" unit, and how the English teachers might make provisions for mastery content. (Social studies and art teachers would add their own appropriate entries by analyzing mastery content in their respective fields.) This chart becomes the basis for making daily plans for each of the units. Figure 17 shows a set of daily plans for the first week of the "American Women" unit, assuming a double-period class meeting, five times a week. Note that these daily plans now make reference to specific reading. Observe as well that detailed lesson-by-lesson planning is necessary since teams of teachers and large groups of students are involved.

All of these materials can be assembled into a unit planning guide which is then added to the notebooks. These unit planning guides would probably include the following materials:

1. A one-page rationale for the course.
2. An outline of the "Themes and Disciplinary Contributions."
3. The "Mastery Content and Unit Placement" chart for each of the contributing disciplines.
4. An "Analysis of Weekly Unit Emphases" for each unit.
5. Learning objectives for the mastery content of each of the disciplines.
6. The daily plans, as developed by the teams.
7. Lists of resources to be used in implementing the units.

Such materials, I believe, enable the teachers to plan interesting interdisciplinary courses that still provide effectively for the mastery content. Note again that it is a "top-down" process that begins with general concepts and provides objectives only where they are needed.

# 14 How to Design
## Sound Elective Programs

One of the effects of the so-called back-to-basics movement seems to be a retreat from elective programs. Many school administrators, responding to the complaints of parents about "easy courses" and taking too seriously the carping of critics such as Paul Copperman (1978), have insisted that English departments return to year-long required courses. Yet Arthur Applebee's (1978) study of a random sample of ninety-six schools from across the nation revealed (p. 62) that there seems to be no wholesale abandonment of elective programs: "Fifty-two percent of the schools reported elective courses for tenth grade students; 78 percent reported electives for twelfth grade students."

The question posed in the chapter title is therefore one that concerns both schools that have elective programs and those that are still interested in developing them. This chapter describes a process of developing elective programs that make specific provisions for mastery content.

We begin by assuming that the processes described in preceding chapters have resulted in identification of the mastery components of the English curriculum. The first question that planners must answer, then, is how to ensure that all students will achieve mastery skills within an elective framework. Here several planning options are possible, which should be examined systematically before courses are developed:

1. *Students will take required courses emphasizing mastery content; when they have passed those required courses, they will be offered a range of electives.* One of the simplest answers to the question of "mastery with options" is this one, where, for example, students would take required English courses in grades 7-9 in which mastery content would be emphasized, and then elect English mini-courses in grades 10-12, with those elective courses simply reviewing mastery content as needed. If this option is chosen, then the process described earlier for identifying mastery content in a planning matrix is used, with the matrix encompassing only those grade

levels where courses are required. The advantage of this method is that it is relatively easy to use and ensures that mastery content will be taught. There are two difficulties with this approach. First, it can result in junior high courses that are heavy with mastery requirements at a time when student interest needs special accommodation. Second, it can result in a decline of competency, because skills need continued reinforcement.

2. *Students will pass a competency test before they are eligible for elective courses.* This solution is a variation of the first; as students enter high school they are given competency tests based on the mastery content; the results are then used to determine whether students will be directed into basic or elective courses. Instituting this approach requires the careful development and validation of the competency tests, since test results will be used for placement. The special advantage of this method is that a valid testing program ensures that mastery has been achieved before the student moves on to more advanced work. The same drawbacks noted above apply here as well: Basic courses can easily become dull and uninspiring, especially for students who are likely to be enrolled in such courses; and a decline in mastery might occur if skills are not consistently reinforced.

3. *Mastery skills will be taught in every elective course.* In this solution, the elective courses provide only a choice of theme to be emphasized; there is no choice of the study of mastery, since mastery content is included in every course. If this solution is chosen, the teachers planning elective courses need to make certain that sufficient provision has been made for study of the mastery component. And, to be effective, this solution requires that three conditions be present. First, the elective courses should be one semester in length, if adequate attention is to be given to both the course theme and mastery content. Second, the scope of the mastery content must be sharply limited so that it does not dominate the elective offering. Third, each teacher of elective courses needs to know how to assess achievement and how to individualize. Since all three conditions rarely occur in any one school, this solution seems to result in the slighting of the mastery content.

4. *Students will be required to take a distribution of elective courses.* This solution also requires careful planning for its successful implementation. First, the distribution sectors must

be identified. Thus, a department might decide to distribute courses among these three sectors: reading and literature; composition and grammar; communication and critical thinking. Next, the mastery content must be allocated to the appropriate distribution sectors. For example, the mapping approach used in Chapter 5 identified eight areas of English: reading and study skills, literature and the mass media, composition, grammar and language study, word study and vocabulary, speaking and listening, critical and creative thinking, and spelling, punctuation, and usage. These eight areas might be distributed among the three sectors in this fashion:

| *Distribution Sector* | *Mastery Areas* |
|---|---|
| 1. Reading and literature | Reading and study skills, literature and the mass media, word study and vocabulary development. |
| 2. Composition and grammar | Composition, grammar and language, spelling, punctuation, and usage. |
| 3. Communication and critical thinking | Speaking and listening, critical and creative thinking. |

As teachers develop elective courses in the distribution sectors, they take pains to ensure that the mastery content from the allocated areas is programmed into each course. The distribution solution seems to be an attractive answer because it results in an easy matching of mastery with options; the main drawback is that it requires special record-keeping to ensure that distribution requirements are in fact being met. Also, teachers need to individualize here as well, so that they aren't teaching mastery content in composition, for example, to students who have already mastered the skills.

One variation of the distribution approach is to develop two or more levels of distribution courses, with mastery content allocated in terms of its difficulty. Thus, a department might develop three kinds of composition and grammar courses: Level 100 courses would include basic mastery elements; level 200 courses, intermediate mastery elements; and level 300, advanced mastery elements. Students would be required to pass a 300-level course in each sector. Obviously, both the planning and the record-keeping are even more complex.

5. *Mastery content is allocated to elective courses according to the school's calendar.* In this approach, the teachers decide, for example, that all elective courses offered during the first quarter will stress composition; second-quarter courses will emphasize reading and study skills; third-quarter courses, grammar and language; and fourth-quarter, speaking and listening. This approach works reasonably well for the first year it is implemented but presents a problem during succeeding years. In each succeeding year, teachers of elective courses must diagnose for the achievement of mastery content and prescribe accordingly.

6. *The first semester (or the first twelve weeks) of each year is devoted to a required course emphasizing mastery content; the rest of the year, students are free to take any electives they wish.* Although this solution is easy to implement, it can again result in heavy required courses that must be endured until more enjoyable electives can be studied.

It should be apparent from the above that there is no best solution to the problem of combining mastery with choice. Each department needs to study the alternatives, weighing whatever constraints are placed by school administrators, and choose the option that makes the best sense to them and their students. Once the decision has been made, they can then follow certain rational steps in planning elective courses. (A useful survey of the planning process and elective offerings can be found in Oliver, 1978.) These steps are briefly summarized here and will be followed by a fuller discussion of the specifics of course planning:

1. Decide on the organizational strategy for providing mastery with options.
2. Confer with administrators on planning constraints—budget, staffing, space, scheduling.
3. Determine which grade levels will be involved in elective courses.
4. Decide on the length of elective courses.
5. Decide whether special instructional systems will be used— team teaching, flexible group size, modular or block scheduling, special instructional approaches.

6. Decide on grouping issues—will students be grouped by grade level, by "phases" or ability level, by interest alone.

7. Survey teacher preferences for kinds of courses they would like to offer.

8. Survey student interests to determine which courses should be offered.

The planning process will result in a list of elective courses to be offered to students. The concern at that point is to develop specific courses that appeal to students and teach the requisite skills. The general nature of the planning—the process by which mastery content is included and units are planned—will, of course, be determined by the decision made at the outset concerning the organizational structure chosen. The specific planning of the course can follow the model described in Chapter 12:

1. Decide on the number and themes of the units.

2. Identify the mastery content to be taught in focused units of study.

3. Allocate integrated mastery content to appropriate thematic units.

4. Identify for each unit the thematic understandings, common readings, mastery content, and organic learnings.

5. Make tentative daily plans on articulating and sequencing the unit outcomes.

And, finally, assemble all of these materials into elective course study guides which can be issued as supplements to the English notebook.

# 15 Writing Mastery Learning Units

Heretofore the terms "mastery curriculum," "mastery skills and concepts," and "mastery content" have been used somewhat interchangeably to refer to curriculum content which, in the view of knowledgeable teachers and scholars, meets two important criteria: (1) it is considered basic or essential for all students, and (2) it requires careful structuring for optimal learning. The following discussion suggests a process for turning this mastery content into "mastery learning units"—units of study developed and implemented according to the principles of mastery learning.

First a definition is in order. James H. Block, one of the most knowledgeable advocates of mastery learning, describes mastery learning as a teaching-learning strategy characterized by these six features:

1. A set of course objectives is specified; students are expected to master these at a high level of achievement.

2. The course is divided into a number of smaller units which teach only a few of the course objectives at a time. (Block recommends units of two weeks in length.)

3. Students are exposed to the unit material in standard fashion and are tested for mastery of the unit's objectives; those who fall below the specified mastery standard are provided with corrective activities.

4. The student's mastery of the course is evaluated as a whole, on the basis of what the student has achieved, not on how well the student has achieved in comparison to classmates.

5. The mastery learning approach can be implemented in a group-based, teacher-paced format or on an individual, self-paced format.

6. It relies primarily on human beings as resources, not on technological devices. (Adapted from Block and Burns, 1977, p. 12.)

Does mastery learning work more effectively than other teaching-learning strategies? In what I consider to be a fair and objective review of the research on mastery learning, Block and Burns (1977, p. 26) conclude as follows:

> The findings of . . . mastery learning research suggest that mastery approaches to instruction do work. The approaches have not yet had as large effects on student learning as their advocates propose are possible, but they have had consistently positive effects. In quantitative terms, mastery approaches have usually produced greater student learning than nonmastery approaches, and they have usually produced relatively less variability in this learning. In qualitative terms, mastery approaches have typically helped students acquire higher order learning, though there is some question as to whether this higher order learning has been retained.

Mastery learning, however, is not without its critics. Probably the most cogent theoretical arguments advanced against it are those of Mueller (1976, p. 51), as expressed in "Mastery Learning: Partly Boon, Partly Boondoggle."

> What the model does not do well—especially when implemented in a traditionally organized school structure . . . is maximize learning for all students. Since the entire instructional emphasis is on a finite set of instructional objectives (those constituting basic skills and knowledges), a learning ceiling is established beyond which the faster students are not allowed to progress. Consequently, the mastery model has limited usefulness in the upper grades . . . and in any instructional units . . . where basic skills and knowledges do not (or should not) constitute a major portion of the total instructional objectives. Further, the mastery model is not useful (in fact is probably dysfunctional) in training students to learn independently. And finally, grades resultant from mastery learning have minimal usefulness in decision making and prediction.

I feel the best rebuttal of Mueller's criticisms comes from Benjamin Bloom. In a private conversation with the author in April 1980, Bloom indicated that he does *not* believe that mastery learning, as he now defines it, should be concerned with a finite set of basic instructional objectives, determined in advance by the teacher—and should *not* be limited to packaged units developed according to some inflexible paradigm. Instead, Bloom believes that classroom teachers should be encouraged to develop their own mastery learning processes and materials, as long as those processes and materials impinge directly on what he terms the "alterable variables" of learning. Bloom's recent research (see, for example, his 1979 monograph) suggests that teachers developing their own mastery learning approaches should keep these guidelines in mind:

1. Check on the cognitive entry characteristics and ensure that students reach adequate levels of competence on these essen-

tial entry behaviors. As Bloom uses the term, cognitive entry characteristics are the specific knowledges, abilities, or skills that are essential for learning a particular task. He finds that such prerequisites correlate +.70 or higher with measures of achievement in a subject.

2. Teach in a way that reflects the basic principles of teaching and learning. Bloom notes that the research on teaching effectiveness suggests that certain behaviors related to the basic characteristics of teaching (cues, reinforcement, participation) are strongly related to pupil achievement, as follows: *cues*—clarity, variety, meaningfulness, and strength of explanations and directions provided by teacher or materials; *reinforcement*—variety, frequency, and individualization of amount and type of reinforcement; *participation*—active participation and engagement in the learning task.

3. Use formative tests to give students frequent feedback about learning and to identify the students who need corrective work. Bloom (1979, p. 7) notes that

> The use of formative tests in this way insures that most of the students have the necessary cognitive prerequisites for each new learning task, that students have increased interest in the learning and greater confidence in their own ability to learn, and that they use more of the classroom time to actively engage in the learning process.

4. Provide the needed correctives to those students who do not achieve mastery levels in the formative tests. Bloom currently places most emphasis on peer tutoring as a corrective device, as opposed to drill sheets and the like.

Bloom has concluded, on the basis of recent research by his doctoral students, that such a flexible model of mastery learning can be used to achieve a broad range of educational outcomes, using a variety of teaching methods (including so-called discovery approaches)—and can achieve those objectives more effectively than conventional teaching methods.

Although a review of recent educational journals suggests that there is much general interest in mastery learning, English educators seem indifferent to the technique. Only one of the studies reviewed by Block and Burns dealt with K-12 English: Okey's (1975) study of mastery learning in primary grades mathematics and language arts. Okey found that in seven measures of achievement, mastery learning yielded scores statistically greater than the scores of nonmastery groups, and in the remaining seven yielded scores greater, but not statistically greater, than scores of nonmastery groups. Further evidence of the lack of interest among English educators is the fact that no specific articles on the subject of mastery learning in English were reported in *Education Index* for 1975 through 1978.

We can only speculate about the reasons for this seeming lack of interest. The likeliest explanation is that English teachers do not believe that the subject of English fits the mastery learning model. However, I believe that mastery learning can be used to good effect in English if certain considerations are kept in mind. First, mastery learning should be used only with the mastery curriculum, although Bloom himself would probably differ with this point of view. Second, I prefer to use the Block and Anderson mastery model with focused mastery units, not integrated mastery learnings. As noted previously, it is desirable to include a number of integrated thematic units in the English curriculum, and the emphasis on inquiry and discussion in integrated units suggests that the structured type of mastery learning approaches might not be applicable here. It should be noted, however, that the more flexible approach suggested recently by Bloom could readily be applied to even thematic units.

Given these cautions, then, here is an explanation of how mastery learning units can be derived from the mastery curriculum, followed by details for developing a composition unit using this approach. The discussion of how to develop a mastery learning unit will be somewhat general; readers interested in a more specific explanation of the mastery learning approach are referred to Block and Anderson's 1975 manual.


## A Mastery Learning Unit for English

Begin by assuming that mastery content for a given grade or level of English has been determined and that the lists of learning objectives have been written. Further assume that you have decided on the number and theme of integrated units, have determined which mastery content should be integrated, and have thus identified a number of focused mastery units for that course. At this point you should review the scope of the focused mastery units so identified, to see if they can be taught within the two-week limit recommended by Block. Two shorter units can be combined into one, or one long unit can be divided into two. In general, however, you will probably find that the focused units previously identified are appropriate in length.

You then proceed to develop the necessary materials which will enable teachers to implement a mastery learning approach with that focused unit. Begin by reviewing the objectives previously identified; you may see fit to modify the previously developed list to make it more comprehensive and specific. Then write an explanation for the teacher, suggesting one or more ways for presenting the basic content to the class, perhaps reminding the teacher of the important learning principles summarized above. The basic presentation methods can include strategies such as lecture, discussion, text, and film; the important point is to apply the principles of cueing, reinforcing, and active participation. The teacher also needs suggestions for assessing cognitive entry characteristics, to ensure that students have the requisite knowledge and skills to begin the unit.

The next step is to develop a diagnostic progress test for each unit. This test, according to Block, should sample the outcomes of the unit, including about twenty or twenty-five objective items. After writing the diagnostic items, prepare an answer key and a set of directions.

The final step in preparing mastery learning materials is to develop a set of what Block calls "correctives"—remediation activities for the students who do not achieve the specified mastery level. The correctives, obviously, should employ teaching-learning activities different from those used in the initial presentation of materials and, as far as possible, should require student involvement and active learning. Block notes that small-group study sessions seem to be most effective as correctives for primary and secondary students. Insofar as possible, the correctives should be keyed to learning objectives and test items on a so-called correctives sheet, so that the student who errs on test item 6, for example, knows that that item is related to the objective "identify noun clause used as subject," and knows that corrective activity 5 will clarify that particular problem.

These materials are then delivered to the teachers who will implement the mastery learning unit:

1. The list of objectives, expanded and clarified if necessary.

2. The one-page statement recommending presentation activities.

3. Reminders about assessing cognitive entry characteristics.

4. The diagnostic progress test, with directions and answer key.

5. The correctives sheet and the necessary corrective materials.

The classroom teacher then implements the unit according to the mastery strategy: The teacher assesses entry characteristics and helps students lacking needed skills to develop them before beginning the unit; presents the unit objectives to the class; gives an overview of the method used in presenting the material; teaches the unit to the class, applying basic learning principles; gives formative feedback and provides the needed correctives.

This "pure" model of the mastery learning approach can be used without modification for learning the concepts, terminology, and facts of language and literature. I believe, however, that it can also be used with some modifications to teach composition effectively. This is how such an approach might work: Assume that you have decided to develop a focused mastery unit on "writing the expository essay" for eighth grade students. You review the list of objectives that was previously developed for the English notebook, as presented in Figure 9.

If these objectives seem satisfactory, your next step is to decide what cognitive entry characteristics are needed in order for the student to write such an essay. You make this determination by asking "Knowing what skills I will teach in this unit, what other important knowledge and skills would an eighth grade student need in order to begin this unit on expository writing?" You assume that your teaching in the unit will focus on the mastery objectives; your list of cognitive entry characteristics will emphasize the general knowledge and skills needed before the mastery objectives can be effectively learned. You might then develop a list of entry characteristics:

1. Can define in own words the concept of "exposition."

2. Can define in own words the concept of "chronological order" and can explain how such an order can be used in planning a shorter essay.

3. Can write sentences that are correct, clear, and of appropriate stylistic maturity.

4. Can write developmental paragraphs that observe the conventions of such paragraphs (unity, coherence, adequate development).

5. Proofreads with due care, paying special attention to spelling, punctuation, and usage.

With this analysis completed, you are ready to prepare the teacher materials which will identify the cognitive entry characteristics and suggest the presentation activities. Figure 18 shows a sample statement.

Note that the suggestions for presentation activities in Figure 18 refer to an "Expository Essay Assignment." A carefully structured assignment sheet is the best way to present the objectives to the student. The sample assignment sheet shown in Figure 19 includes four kinds of information:

1. The assignment. This spells out in specific terms the nature of the composition assignment, including some comments designed to stimulate student interest.

2. Objectives. This is a list of the objectives, written in terms the student can understand.

3. Standards. This indicates the standards by which the student will be judged and the grades assigned.

4. Major errors. This lists the errors which, for students in this grade level, are considered to be of major importance.

Observe that three grades are suggested in composition mastery units: *A*, *B*, and *I*. The students should learn that any paper which does not achieve mastery standards will be considered incomplete and that certain corrective activities must be completed before the paper is resubmitted. In a sense the composition is the diagnostic progress test.

The composition correctives are then prepared. First it is suggested that you mimeograph forms similar to the "Mastery Assignment Grading Form" shown in Figure 20. Note that the form specifies the objectives, providing space for both a student self-assessment and the teacher's evaluation. The form also lists the "major errors" categories, with space for teacher- and self-assessment. Space is also provided for both the student and the teacher to enter one of the three grades. If the student has earned a grade of *B*, the student is expected to correct the mistakes on the original and record the errors in a notebook for future reference. If a grade of *I* is given, the student is expected to take the corrective action before resubmitting the paper. Three standard correctives are listed on the form, as these are likely to be used most often. For serious problems of content, thought, or lack of development the student is expected to confer with the teacher or one of the good writers in the class, who serves as a writing tutor. Only an intelligent writer can help with such problems. For problems of organization, sentence structure, and paragraphing, a small group self-help session is suggested. Block recommends that these self-help groups be composed of students who failed to achieve mastery for very different reasons. Thus, the composition small group might include one student who organized poorly, another who wrote clumsy sentences, and a third who had trouble with paragraphing. The expectation is that they will be able to help each other.

For specific errors in usage, sentence correctness, spelling, and punctuation, the student is directed to a corrective exercise. These are mimeographed sheets on file in the classroom, English resource center, or writing laboratory. Each sheet deals with a specific error, is keyed to a commonly used correction symbol, and uses a format like the one shown in Figure 21. The student is expected to complete the corrective exercise form and staple it to the revised composition.

### Using Error Analysis

Teachers who dislike such highly structured correctives may prefer to use a process that David Drost (1979) calls "error analysis." The student is expected to explain why each error marked is in fact an error and supplies a corrected example. The important point is to be sure that major errors are corrected.

These prepared materials should help the teacher do an effective job of assessing entry characteristics and teaching the unit skills. There are three places in the writing process where the teacher can provide for formative feedback, depending upon the teacher's preferences. First, the teacher can monitor the students' progress as they do their first drafts, if the writing is done in class, giving students appropriate reinforcement and suggesting alternative approaches to the topic. Second, when the first draft has been completed, the teacher can set up peer editing groups in which peers give the writer specific feedback about mastery of the objectives. The peers can use the Mastery Assignment Grading Form shown in Figure 20. Finally, the teacher's feedback on the final draft of the essay provided on the grading form should give the student the information needed to make improvement.

Developing such carefully structured composition mastery units does not mean that all writing will be done in this mode. There will always be a need for spontaneous writing, for unstructured expressive writing, and for creative writing. And there should always be a place for integrated English language arts units where the writing grows out of a need to communicate about the theme of that unit. Nevertheless, mastery learning can be of help with the right kind of content.

# 16 A Personal Epilogue: A Curriculum of Meaning

Up to this point this work has emphasized the process and form of curriculum work in English, to the neglect of content and substance. I have indicated that such neglect is intentional as I value the ability of school-based leaders and teachers to make their own determinations about content and emphases. However, I would like to close with a brief personal statement on these neglected issues because I feel strongly about them.

The challenge of the 1980s, as I view this emerging decade, is for concerned educational leaders in the field of English to develop a curriculum of meaning that will help young people learn how to discover and create meaning for themselves. Let me at the outset contrast the curriculum of meaning with the curriculum of competence, since competence seems to be in the saddle.

A curriculum of competence supports the utilitarian. It is the curriculum advocated by those who favor competency-based education, who would define the English curriculum as a collection of applied skills—filling out forms, making a telephone call, applying for a job. I do not question the need for competence, and I would not criticize leaders or teachers who use such practical applications as means of motivating the uninterested or who reluctantly respond to state mandates—and I hope that I have suggested means by which leaders and teachers can make a reasonable response to such mandates.

However, I question the effectiveness of a competency-based curriculum on three grounds. First, such a curriculum unwisely emphasizes discrete skills—and those discrete skills are not sufficiently generalizable. Our students would gain more power by mastering a few cognitive processes of high transferability, rather than by trying to master numerous discrete applications. A student who has learned to think critically, to read with understanding and insight, and to speak and write effectively can successfully handle an unlimited number of specific tasks requiring the application of those skills.

Second, undue emphasis on competency can trivialize the English curriculum, for its emphasis on assessment might encourage teachers to stress such less important matters as comma placement, capitalization, and letter forms. The best competency tests, of course, measure the more general communication skills, but too many tests that I have examined or have heard described give prominence to the assessment of the less important but more measurable skills. A teacher who is confronted with such tests will understandably stress such items in the taught curriculum.

The third difficulty is that too many of the competencies are derived from an analysis of what an adult needs in order to "survive," instead of from an analysis of what young people need in order to grow. One middle-school teacher in Florida put it to me this way: "I'm so busy teaching my eighth graders how to keep a checkbook that I don't have time to teach literature. How many eighth graders do you know who have their own checkbooks?" I believe instead, that all young people need to learn how to make sense out of their lives—and that an English curriculum of meaning can make a major contribution toward achieving this goal.

What might be the specific attributes of a curriculum of meaning? In literature it would minimize the analysis of literary genres and stress instead the meaning perceived through the writer's vision. It would deemphasize the ephemera of popular culture for all except the least able and would emphasize instead the meaningful works of both present and past, to the extent that they are accessible to the young. It would also provide time for the careful analysis of television and film since these media are so central in young people's lives—and the ability to view critically seems to be a major part of meaning-making. Such a curriculum would also attach importance to the generalizable skills of critical reading, to help young people become more skilled in evaluating the printed messages that bombard them. In short, it would stress the meaning of literature—and the literature of meaning.

In language study the curriculum of meaning would have little to do with word classes and sentence patterns, except as such taxonomic concerns are necessary to establish a common vocabulary and to appease parents. But it would help students understand the structure of English, would place appropriate emphasis on the history of language, and would stress the relationship between language and meaning. And it would be centrally concerned with the particular ways in which language can both inform and confuse, persuade and repel, inspire and enrage.

An English curriculum of meaning would also accentuate a composing process that derives from the need to understand and express meaning. Such writing becomes a way of knowing, as the young writer struggles to discover and communicate meaning in all forms of discourse. Such a composition curriculum would, of course, give appropriate attention to the applied writing skills which the student needs as a consumer, worker, and citizen—but it would place much more emphasis on the writing skills and processes needed by the student as a person. The person-centered processes are concerned with what one knows—how to discover that core of knowledge and increase its realm, how to communicate what one knows—and with the centrality of writing in all those processes.

I believe that a curriculum of meaning would include mastery units in critical and creative thinking, which would teach students how to use creative problem-solving strategies in identifying problems, devising solutions, and communicating answers. Such units are typically excluded from the English curriculum since they seem not to be primarily concerned with communication. But I would argue that critical and creative thinking is the foundation of effective communication.

Finally, as noted previously, I think the English curriculum should provide adequate time for integrated thematic units that help students, under the direction of a caring and competent teacher, use these meaning-centered skills in examining issues grounded in the human condition. In perhaps imperceptible ways, such units can make special a contribution to meaning-finding and meaning-making.

Obviously, such a curriculum of meaning can best come into being as committed instructional leaders work with teachers to translate general principles into specific decisions regarding selection, organization, and placement of the components. I hope this guide has been of help to my colleagues as they grapple with those decisions.

# Figures

Period of
Curriculum History

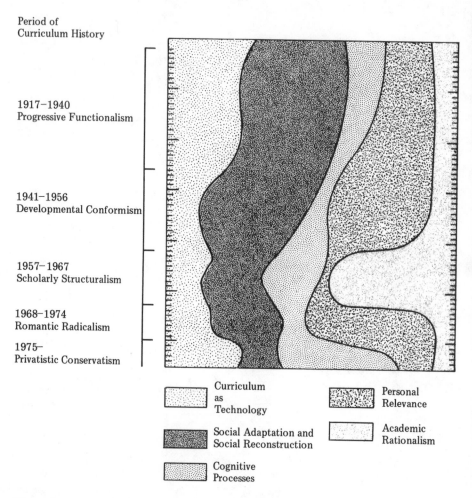

1917–1940
Progressive Functionalism

1941–1956
Developmental Conformism

1957–1967
Scholarly Structuralism

1968–1974
Romantic Radicalism

1975–
Privatistic Conservatism

Curriculum
as
Technology

Personal
Relevance

Social Adaptation and
Social Reconstruction

Academic
Rationalism

Cognitive
Processes

Figure 1.  Relationship of the Five Basic Curriculum Streams.

| Step | Personnel Involved | Date |
|---|---|---|
| 1. Determine need; identify parameters, resources, responsibilities | Instructional leader, district administrators | May |
| 2. Inform English teachers, solicit their cooperation | Instructional leader, English faculty | May, September |
| 3. Brief the district leadership about mastery theory; determine whether theory will govern curriculum development | Instructional leader, administrators | June |
| 4. Select task force, advisory council, writing team; confer with advisory council for their input | Instructional leader, district administrators | September |
| 5. Collect and tally mapping data | Instructional leader, task force | October |
| 6. Develop preliminary version of content planning matrix | Instructional leader, task force | November |
| 7. Evaluate planning matrix; make appropriate modifications | Instructional leader, task force, advisory council, consultant | December–February |
| 8. Meet with teachers to revise matrix, determine format of guides | Instructional leader | March–April |
| 9. Prepare writing team for writing course objectives | Instructional leader, writing team | May |
| 10. Monitor writing team | Instructional leader, writing team | July |
| 11. Check course objectives against course offerings | Instructional leader | August |
| 12. Determine plans for future development of materials | Instructional leader, district administrators | August |

Figure 2. A Planning Calendar for Curriculum Development.

| | Mastery | Organic | Team-Planned | Student-Determined |
|---|---|---|---|---|
| 1. Basic orientation | Cognitive processes; academic rationalism; technology | Personal relevance | Social adaptation and reconstruction; academic rationalism | Personal relevance |
| 2. Developed by | District leaders with teacher input | Classroom teacher | Teaching teams | Classroom teacher and student |
| 3. Supported by | District curriculum guides | In-service training | Team-planned units | Teacher- and student-made materials |
| 4. Use of learning objectives | Extensive | None | Some | None |
| 5. Importance of text | Much | Little | Some | None |
| 6. Testing | Systematic assessment through objective measures on a district-wide basis | Observation and diagnosis by classroom teacher | Team-developed tests | No tests |
| 7. Importance of district articulation and coordination | Much | None | Some | None |

Figure 3. Salient Characteristics of Four Types of Curricula.

Teacher's Code No. __11-3__          Grade __11__          Ability Group __—__          School __Central High__

Instructions: In the appropriate columns below, please note the mastery skills and concepts you ordinarily teach in a given year. It is not important that the skills or concepts be listed in the order in which they are taught. Do not include enrichment learnings or those you consider "organic."

| Reading and Study Skills | Literature and the Media (include longer works used for class study) | Composition | Grammar and Language | Word Study and Vocabulary | Speaking and Listening | Critical and Creative Thinking | Spelling, Punctuation, and Usage | Other |
|---|---|---|---|---|---|---|---|---|
| main idea<br>making inferences<br>dictionary | major periods of American literature<br>symbolism<br>naturalism<br>realism<br>*Huckleberry Finn*<br>*The Scarlet Letter*<br>*Red Badge of Courage*<br>O'Neill's plays<br>*Death of a Salesman* | paragraph skills<br>sentence combining<br>expository essay<br>book review<br>persuasive essay | review parts of speech<br>major American dialects<br>history of American language | verbal analogies<br>roots and prefixes<br>SAT word lists | class discussions<br>making introductions<br>college and job interviews<br>short formal speech | analysis of advertising | review spelling and punctuation as needed | |

Figure 4. Curriculum Project: English Language Arts. Mapping Form for Curriculum Mastery Elements, Central School District.

| Components | Grade 7 | | | Grade 8 | | | Grade 9 | |
| --- | --- | --- | --- | --- | --- | --- | --- | --- |
| | North Middle School | South Middle School | West Middle School | North | South | West | Washington High | Lincoln High |
| Word Classes | n-11<br>v-11<br>av-11<br>aj-11 | | n-111prep-11<br>v-111det-111<br>av-11con-111<br>aj-11pro-111 | prep-1n-11<br>art-11v-1<br>con-11av-1<br>pro-1adj-111 | n-111prep-11<br>v-11art-1111<br>av-11con-111<br>aj-111pro-11 | | n-1111  prep-1111<br>v-1111  con-1111<br>av-1111  det-1111<br>aj-1111  pro-1111 | |
| Sentence Parts | | | | | | | | |
| Sentence Patterns, Types | | | | | | | | |
| Phonology | | | | | | | | |
| Morphology | | | | | | | | |
| Dialect Study | | | | | | | | |
| Language History | | | | | | | | |
| Other: | | | | | | | | |

Figure 5. Curriculum Project: English Language Arts. Analysis Form for Grammar and Language Mastery Element, Central School District.

| Evaluation Issue | Process | Agent |
|---|---|---|
| *Focus* | | |
| 1. Are only mastery elements included, and organic and enrichment components excluded? | Analyze mastery concept, mapping data | Instructional leader, consultant, staff |
| *Orientation* | | |
| 2. Does the content reflect a syncretic orientation, drawing from analyses of the four substantive orientations? | Analyze subject, cognitive processes, student, society | Instructional leader, task force |
| *Response to External Requirements* | | |
| 3. Are basic competencies mandated by state or local district provided for? | Identify state or local competencies; analyze mapping data | Instructional leader, task force |
| 4. Does the curriculum respond adequately to the reasonable expectations of parents, local employers, community? | Identify and discuss expectations; analyze mapping data | Instructional leader, advisory council |
| 5. Is there a satisfactory match between the elements of the curriculum and the items included in standardized tests used in the district? | Analyze tests and mapping data | Instructional leader, task force |
| *Research Base* | | |
| 6. Does the taught curriculum reflect the best current knowledge about the learner and the subject? | Review research data; analyze mapping data | Instructional leader, consultant, task force |
| *Comprehensiveness and Articulation* | | |
| 7. Within a given area of the English curriculum, does the sequence of skills and concepts from grade to grade seem to follow some coherent and acceptable plan? | Review sequence options; analyze mapping data along the graded continuum | Instructional leader, task force |
| 8. At a given grade level, do the several areas of the curriculum exhibit complementarity, where such complementarity seems appropriate? | Analyze mapping data from area to area at a given grade level | Instructional leader, task force |
| 9. Is there sufficient uniformity among schools at the same level to ensure efficiency and consistency of results? | Analyze mapping data from separate schools | Instructional leader, task force |
| 10. Does the curriculum include all important learning, with no significant omissions? | Analyze mapping data | Instructional leader, task force |
| 11. Does the curriculum provide for adequate reinforcement of important learning without excessive repetition? | Analyze mapping data | Instructional leader, task force |
| 12. From grade to grade, is there a reasonable balance (considering the students' maturity) in terms of the number of important concepts and skills to be learned? | Analyze mapping data from grade to grade | Instructional leader, task force |

Figure 6.  Evaluating the Content Planning Matrix.

| Strand | 7 | 8 | 9 | 10 | 11 | 12 |
|---|---|---|---|---|---|---|
| The Word | Effective and correct words | Appropriateness and clarity | Connotation, denotation; abstract and concrete words | Guidelines for effective word choice | Words for school and career | Words and the writer's purpose |
| The Sentence | Sentence parts and patterns; combining basic patterns | Developing the basic patterns; combining with grammatical structures | Clarity, economy, and variety in sentence use; sentence combining | Sentence combining; improved sentences | Writing effective sentences through combining strategies | Developing a mature style |
| The Paragraph | The nature of the paragraph | Types of paragraphs and their development | Writing paragraphs from personal and print sources | Paragraph patterns | Solving paragraph problems | The rhetoric of the paragraph |
| Personal Writing | Creating a story | Observing your world | Using your experiences | Creating a biography | Picturing people and places | Explaining a world |
| Writing about Literature | Responding to literature | Writing the library paper | Reviewing nonfiction | Writing about novels | Writing the research paper | Responding to poetry |
| Argumentation | Expressing an opinion | Defending an opinion | Using persuasion | Writing effective persuasive essays | Writing argumentation | Developing effective arguments |
| Exposition | Giving directions; explaining a process | Explaining your world | Writing a causal analysis | Writing the essay of classification | Making comparisons and contrasts | Combining expository types and skills |
| Applied Writing Skills | The friendly letter; the business letter | Letters of criticism and appreciation; the social note; order forms | Letters for career information; letters to public officials; the note of appreciation | Letters of application; the job application; invitations | Letters for college and career; the college application; writing the career paper | Technical writing; the resume; the letter of application; formal invitations |
| Writing across the Curriculum | School paragraphs | School essays | Library paper; essay tests | Reporting on investigations; essay answers | Biographical research; essay answers | Teacher questions |

**Figure 7. Content Planning Matrix: Composition, Mastery.**

| Orientation | Criteria<br>The English curriculum should . . . | Accept,<br>Mastery | Acceptance<br>Accept,<br>Organic | Accept,<br>Team-<br>Planned | Not<br>Accepted |
|---|---|---|---|---|---|
| Personal<br>Relevance | 1. Include the reading and discussion of contemporary adolescent literature. | | | | |
| | 2. Include the reading and discussion of work written by authors whose ethnic identity is similar to the students'. | | | | |
| | 3. Give the students an opportunity to investigate the folklore and dialect of their region. | | | | |
| | 4. Use selected works from the popular culture for purposes of comparison and motivation. | | | | |
| | 5. Provide for extensive opportunity to use oral language in the classroom. | | | | |
| | 6. Encourage the student to respond personally to literature. | | | | |
| | 7. Help the student value one's individual language. | | | | |
| | 8. Provide extensive opportunities for the student to write personally and expressively. | | | | |
| | 9. Provide time for the discussion of ideas and problems considered relevant and important to the student. | | | | |
| | 10. Help the student think reflectively about personal values. | | | | |
| Cognitive<br>Processes | 1. Help the student use oral language to communicate appropriately and effectively. | | | | |
| | 2. Help the student use written language to communicate effectively in a variety of situations. | | | | |

3. Help the student develop the skills of reading comprehension.

4. Help the student develop the skills of critical reading.

5. Help the student learn to listen attentively and critically.

6. Help the student learn to reason logically.

7. Provide opportunities for the student to find problems and to learn to state problems clearly and accurately.

8. Help the student learn how to retrieve, evaluate, and apply information in the solution of problems.

9. Provide opportunities for the student to think creatively and to generate alternative and innovative solutions.

10. Help the student understand the close relationship between language and thinking, and use basic language analysis skills in evaluating and sending messages.

Social
Adaptation
and
Reconstruction

1. Provide opportunities for the investigation and discussion of socially relevant problems.

2. Provide opportunities for the student to apply language and communication skills in studying the local community.

3. Equip the student with the communication skills needed to function successfully as a citizen, consumer, and worker.

4. Equip the student with the thinking and communicating skills needed to influence local and national policies.

5. Increase the student's understanding of the language and literature of other cultures.

6. Increase the student's understanding of how American language and literature reflect cultural values.

7. Help the student understand the relationship between changes in the society and changes in the language.

8. Help the student eliminate traces of sexism and racism in language.

9. Help the student develop an acceptance and appreciation of the language and literature of other ethnic groups.

10. Help the student develop the skills of evaluating and criticizing the mass media.

Academic Rationalism

1. Help the student develop the ability to interpret literary works.

2. Increase the student's appreciation of literature.

3. Include the reading and study of certain literary classics.

4. Help the student understand the history of British and American literature.

5. Help the student understand English grammar.

6. Help the student understand the function and characteristics of language.

7. Help the student understand the nature and use of nonverbal communication systems.

8. Include the study of the history of the English language.

Figure 8. Comprehensive Criteria for a Syncretic English Curriculum.

*Component:* Expository Writing (04)

*General Skill:* Explaining a process: In a short expository essay, explain some process or skill you know from first-hand experience; explain that process or skill to an audience you identify. (01)

*Course Objectives:*

0820401-1 Select appropriate topic for such an essay, specifying the audience.

2 Develop a useful plan for the essay based on chronological order.

3 Begin the essay effectively.

4 Identify skills, materials, equipment, or special preparations required for the process or skill.

5 Explain steps or processes clearly, in chronological sequence.

6 Define and illustrate any terms not likely to be known by audience.

7 Provide sufficient detail in terms of audience's knowledge and interest.

8 Conclude the essay effectively.

Comments: Two points are important here. First, the student is expected to explain some limited skill or process known from first-hand experience. Second, the student should make a specific attempt to adapt to an identified audience.

Figure 9. Mastery Objectives Form.

| Mastery Skill and Concept: Composition | Focused Unit | Integrated Units | | | |
| --- | --- | --- | --- | --- | --- |
| | | The Spirit of Sports | Choosing a Career | The Black Experience | Divorce and Separation |
| Open sentence combining | X | | | | |
| Eliminating paragraph problems | | incidental emphasis | | incidental emphasis | X |
| Expository essay: classifying and dividing | | | X | | |
| Persuasive essay: solving a problem and selling the solution | X | | | | |
| Writing an interpretation of fiction | | | | X | incidental emphasis |
| Using order blanks and writing order letters | X | | | | |
| Answering essay questions | | X | incidental emphasis | | |

Figure 10. Unit Planning Chart.

| | 1 | 2 | 3 | 4 | 5 | 6 | 7 | 8 | 9 | 10 | 11 | 12 | 13 | 14 | 15 | Notes |
|---|---|---|---|---|---|---|---|---|---|---|---|---|---|---|---|---|
| **Thematic Understandings** | | | | | | | | | | | | | | | | |
| 1. Know extent of divorce | E | | | | | | | | | | | | | | | |
| 2. Know causes of divorce | E | | | | | R | | | | R | | | R | | | stress complexity |
| 3. Know problems caused by divorce | E | | | | | | R | | | R | | | R | | | avoid blaming parents |
| 4. Understand traditional and contemporary values | | E | E | | | R | R | | | R | R | R | R | | | |
| 5. Know how divorce is handled in other cultures | | | | E | | | | | | | | | | | | |
| **Common Readings** | | | | | | | | | | | | | | | | |
| 1. *A Doll's House* | | | | | | E | E | E | E | E | | | | | | assign first week |
| 2. Shakespeare's sonnet | | | | | | | | | | | E | | | | | |
| 3. Carly Simon song | | | | | | | | | | | | E | | | | |
| 4. Selected articles | E | E | E | E | R | | | | | | | | | | | |
| 5. Videotape of "soap opera" | | | | | | | | | | | | E | E | | | |
| **Integrated Mastery Concepts, Skills** | | | | | | | | | | | | | | | | |
| 1. Close reading of nonfiction | | E | E | R | R | | | | | R | R | | | | | |
| 2. Understand literary symbols | | | | | | E | | | | R | | | | | | |
| 3. Eliminate paragraph problems | | | | | E | | | | | | | | | E | | |
| **Organic Learnings** | | | | | | | | | | | | | | | | |
| 1. Accept, cope with feelings | | | E | | | | R | R | R | | | | | | | |
| 2. Express feelings | | E | E | | | | R | R | R | | | R | | E | | |
| 3. Be open to other viewpoints | | E | E | E | E | | | | | | | | | | R | |

**Figure 11.** Unit Outcomes Chart.

*Directions:* Listed below are several possible goals for the courses in the humanities. Read each statement carefully and then answer in two ways. First, tell how important you consider that goal to be for humanities courses in your school by circling one of these numbers:

1. Of no importance at all
2. Of very limited importance
3. Uncertain

4. Of moderate importance
5. Of great importance

Second, tell to what extent you think this goal is being achieved by the humanities courses in your school by circling one of these numbers:

1. Not at all
2. To a very limited extent
3. Uncertain

4. To a moderate extent
5. To a great extent

Check to indicate your position: _____ Teacher of humanities courses
_____ Administrator
_____ Teacher of courses other
than humanities
_____ Student
_____ Parent
_____ Other

| Goals: Courses in the Humanities should help students . . . | How important is this goal? | To what extent is this goal being achieved? |
|---|---|---|
| 1. Understand the history and nature of the American culture. | 1 2 3 4 5 | 1 2 3 4 5 |
| 2. Understand the history and nature of other cultures. | 1 2 3 4 5 | 1 2 3 4 5 |
| 3. Appreciate great works of literature, art, and music from the past. | 1 2 3 4 5 | 1 2 3 4 5 |
| 4. Develop the ability to communicate effectively in writing. | 1 2 3 4 5 | 1 2 3 4 5 |
| 5. Develop the ability to read closely and critically. | 1 2 3 4 5 | 1 2 3 4 5 |
| 6. Learn how to evaluate conflicting historical sources. | 1 2 3 4 5 | 1 2 3 4 5 |
| 7. Use specific facts about a historical period to develop valid generalizations about that period. | 1 2 3 4 5 | 1 2 3 4 5 |
| 8. Deal with conflicts of principle or judgment in a mature way. | 1 2 3 4 5 | 1 2 3 4 5 |

9. Use their knowledge of the past to
achieve a deeper understanding of
the present.    1 2 3 4 5    1 2 3 4 5

10. Use insights and approaches from
various disciplines to understand
important contemporary issues.    1 2 3 4 5    1 2 3 4 5

11. Perceive the interrelation of the fine
arts, literature, history, and philosophy.    1 2 3 4 5    1 2 3 4 5

12. Understand the special way in which
each discipline examines questions and
arrives at its own understanding of truth.    1 2 3 4 5    1 2 3 4 5

13. Develop alternative visions of the future
and understand how those visions are
related to choices made in the present.    1 2 3 4 5    1 2 3 4 5

14. Use a knowledge of artistic structures
and devices to understand the under-
lying meaning of great works of art.    1 2 3 4 5    1 2 3 4 5

15. Become more discriminating in their
choice of and response to contemporary
popular culture.    1 2 3 4 5    1 2 3 4 5

16. Express themselves creatively in one
of the artistic media.    1 2 3 4 5    1 2 3 4 5

17. Become more critical and analytical
in their response to mass media.    1 2 3 4 5    1 2 3 4 5

18. Understand and value their own
ethnic identity.    1 2 3 4 5    1 2 3 4 5

19. Develop an interest in and enthusiasm
for studying the humanities.    1 2 3 4 5    1 2 3 4 5

20. Value the unique contribution of their
own religion and understand the major
teachings of other religions.    1 2 3 4 5    1 2 3 4 5

Figure 12. Sample Form for Evaluating High School Humanities Offerings.

| Grade | Primary Organizational Mode | If Correlated or Interdisciplinary, Which Subjects? | If Correlated, Interdisciplinary, or Isolated, What Is the Major Emphasis? | English Major Emphasis | Social Studies Major Emphasis | Religion Major Emphasis |
|---|---|---|---|---|---|---|
| 9 | Interdisciplinary | English, Social Studies, Religion, Art | A Cross-Cultural Study of Humanities in Contemporary Life | Contemporary Literature | Anthropology: Non-Western Cultures | Non-Western Religions |
| 10 | Interdisciplinary | English, Social Studies, Religion, Art | American Studies | American Literature | American History | Catholicism in America |
| 11 | Correlated | English, Social Studies, Art, Religion | Western Civilization, the Early Periods | Literature of Greece, Rome, Middle Ages | From Egypt to the Middle Ages | Catholic Roots |
| 12 | Articulated | | | Advanced Placement English | Advanced Placement History | Values and Moral Choices |

Figure 13. Sample Chart Listing Recommendations for Humanities Offerings.

Title of Course: Humanities in Contemporary American Life

| Unit Themes | English | Social Studies | Art |
|---|---|---|---|
| Violence in America | | | |
| Persistence in Virtue | | | |
| American Heroes and Heroines | | | |
| American Women | The Struggle for Freedom: Literary Accounts of Liberation | Historical Roots of Sexism in the United States | The American Woman as Artist: The Art of Romaine Brooks |
| American Family | | | |
| Working in the United States | | | |
| Love, American Style | | | |
| American Youth | | | |
| Sports as Myth | | | |
| Black Voices | | | |
| The New Hispanics | | | |
| Poverty and Affluence in the United States | | | |

Figure 14. Sample Chart of Themes and Disciplinary Contributions.

| Mastery Concept or Skill | Violence | Virtue | Heroes | Women | Family | Working | Love | Youth | Sports | Blacks | Hispanics | Poverty |
|---|---|---|---|---|---|---|---|---|---|---|---|---|
| Open Sentence Combining | FML | | | | | | | | | | | |
| Eliminating Paragraph Problems | | | IML | | | | | | | | | |
| Classification Essay | | | | | | | | | IML | | | |
| Selling-a-Solution Essay | | | | | | | | | | | | IML |
| Writing Order Letter | | | | | | FML | | | | | | |
| Answering Essay Questions | | | | | | | | | | | IML | |

Figure 15.  Sample Chart of Mastery Content and Unit Placement in English.

| Week | Category | English | Social Studies | Art |
|---|---|---|---|---|
| 1 | Thematic Understandings | | Historical roots of sexism in the United States | |
| | Supporting Learnings | Expressions of sexism in American literature | | Images of women in early American art |
| | Integrated Mastery | Close reading of factual prose | | |
| | Focused Mastery | | | |
| 2 | Thematic Understandings | The struggle for freedom: literary portraits | The historical context of the struggle against sexism | |
| | Supporting Learnings | | | Visualizing the portraits of women |
| | Integrated Mastery | Understanding the literary symbol | | |
| | Focused Mastery | Sentence combining skills | | |
| 3 | Thematic Understandings | | | Women as artists in the United States: Romaine Brooks |
| | Supporting Learnings | Sexism in the American language | Social forces militating against recognition of women artists | |
| | Integrated Mastery | Paragraph problems | | |
| | Focused Mastery | | | |

Figure 16. Sample Analysis of Weekly Interdisciplinary Unit Emphases on "American Women."

| HOUR | MONDAY | TUESDAY | WEDNESDAY | THURSDAY | FRIDAY |
|---|---|---|---|---|---|
| 9:00–9:30 | Large group presentation: "The European Heritage—Imported Sexism" Guest speaker from *NOW* | Large group: "The Frontier and Its Effect on Sexism" Film followed by lecture | Large group: "The Factory System and Sexism" Student dramatic skit | Large group: "Churches and Sexism in American Life" Panel discussion with clergy | Large group: "Male Apologists for Male Sexism" Students role-playing figures from history |
| 9:30–10:00 | Small groups: Discuss ideas presented in lecture, following prepared discussion guide | Directed independent study: learning package on "Frontier Women" | Small Groups: Discuss influence of factory system, using discussion guide | Class groups: Use packet "Close Reading of Factual Prose" to analyze article on the sexist church | Class groups: Use packet on "Close Reading" to analyze Mailer article |
| 10:00–10:30 | Class groups: Discuss *Huckleberry Finn* excerpt | Class groups: Discuss *Life with Father* excerpt | Large group: Illustrated lecture: "Images of Women in Early American Art" | Small groups: Discuss contemporary images of women in ads | Class groups: Summary and review |

Figure 17. Sample Outline of Daily Plans for an Interdisciplinary Unit on American Women, Week 1.

I. *Assess cognitive entry characteristics.*

Before presenting the unit, be sure that students possess these basic abilities:

1. Can define in own words the concept of "exposition."
2. Can define in own words the concept of "chronological order" and can explain how such an order can be used in planning a shorter essay.
3. Can write sentences that are correct, clear, and of appropriate stylistic maturity.
4. Can write developmental paragraphs that observe the conventions of such paragraphs (unity, coherence, adequate development).
5. Proofreads with due care, paying special attention to spelling, punctuation, and usage.

You can assess these entry characteristics through a brief quiz, class discussion, or brief writing sample. Be sure that students have these skills before presenting the unit.

II. *Present the unit, applying sound teaching and learning principles.*

1. Remember the importance of prewriting. Use one or more of the following prewriting activities:

   a. Stress the importance of sharing what we know. Discuss with the class whether they would like to publish a class collection of "how-to-do-it" essays.
   b. Develop a class "Inventory of Expertness." On a large chart, list the names of students in the class. Each student notes a personal area of expertise.
   c. Have students discuss in small groups what they know best, and what would make the best topics for expository essays.
   d. Ask one student from each group to make a brief oral presentation on a process.

2. Distribute the "Expository Essay Assignment" and discuss it with the students. Give special attention to the objectives and the mastery standards.

3. Teach the essential skills before students are asked to carry out the assignment. Use one or more of the following approaches:

   a. Assign for outside reading Chapter 7 of the text *Composition Skills, Book 2*, published by Science Research Associates. Discuss each section in class after students have read it.
   b. Explain the essential skills to the students, using appropriate models. Stress the following: selecting an appropriate topic, identifying an audience, organizing the essay, using a chronological order, achieving clarity in developmental paragraphs, beginning the essay effectively, adapting to an audience.
   c. Write a sample essay together with the class, taking them through the steps one at a time.

Figure 18. Sample Statement on a Mastery Learning Unit: Writing the Expository Essay—Suggestions to the Teacher.

*The assignment:* You are an expert about many things—how to play a certain sport, how to do some craft or hobby, how to make something, how to achieve some school or personal goal. Identify some process that you know especially well. Choose an audience for whom you would like to write. Then write an essay explaining that process as you know it. If you have trouble thinking of a topic, complete this statement: "I know how to...." The essay should contain four to six paragraphs.

*Objectives:* Your essay should demonstrate that you know how to achieve the following writing objectives:

1. Select an appropriate topic for the essay and identify the audience.
2. Develop a useful plan for the essay, using a chronological order.
3. Begin the essay effectively so that it arouses interest and makes clear the main idea.
4. Identify the skills, materials, equipment, or special preparations required for the process.
5. Explain the steps clearly in the order in which they are done.
6. Define and illustrate any terms not likely to be clear to the audience.
7. Provide enough detail in terms of the audience's knowledge and interest.
8. Conclude the essay effectively.

*Standards:* Your essay will be read with the above objectives in mind. In addition, you will be expected to show that you can write an essay reasonably free of major errors. You will be given one of three grades:

$A =$  This paper is an excellent paper. It demonstrates that all the objectives have been met, that the writing has a personal style, and that the paper is free of major errors.

$B =$  This paper is a good paper. It demonstrates that the most important writing objectives have been met, that the style is clear, and that there are no more than four major errors.

$I =$  This paper is considered incomplete. It does not demonstrate the mastery of the writing objectives and/or contains more than four major errors. Do the necessary corrective activities and submit a revised paper.

*Major errors:* For purposes of this assignment, a major error is one of the following, indicated by the symbol noted:

$S =$  A word is misspelled.
$Fr =$  A fragment or piece of a sentence has been written as a sentence.
$R =$  Two sentences have been run together with incorrect punctuation.
$US =$  A basic error in usage has been made.
$¶ =$  An error in paragraphing has been made, or a paragraph has not been fully developed.

Figure 19. Sample Assignment Sheet for Writing the Expository Essay.

Student's Name _____John Walker_____ Teacher _____Mr. Williams_____

Mastery Assignment _____Expository Essay: Explaining a Process_____

| *Mastery Objectives:* Does your essay . . . | Your Evaluation | Your Teacher's Evaluation |
|---|---|---|
| 1. Develop an appropriate topic? | yes | yes |
| 2. Use a clear plan with chronological order? | yes | no |
| 3. Begin effectively? | yes | no |
| 4. Identify skills needed? | yes | yes |
| 5. Explain steps clearly? | yes | yes |
| 6. Define and illustrate terms? | yes | no |
| 7. Provide enough detail for audience? | yes | yes |
| 8. Conclude effectively? | yes | yes |

| *Major Errors:* How many of these major errors did you make? | Your Count | Teacher's Count |
|---|---|---|
| *Spelling* | 0 | 2 |
| *Run-ons* | 0 | 0 |
| *Fragments* | 0 | 1 |
| *Usage* | 0 | 2 |

*Grade:* Your grade ___B___ Your teacher's grade ___I___

*Teacher's Comments:*

> You did an excellent job of identifying the skills and explaining the steps. I think you gave just the right amount of detail, so that even I learned something about watching pro-football—and I thought I was an expert. However, as shown above, you did not meet three of the objectives and made too many major errors.

*Correctives Recommended for Incomplete Papers:*

_____ Confer with the teacher

___X___ Work with a classmate who achieved all the objectives

___X___ Complete corrective exercise

_____ Other _____

Figure 20. Sample Mastery Assignment Grading Form.

*Fr:* This symbol in your composition means that you have written a piece of a sentence and have punctuated it as a sentence.

*Explanation of the Error:* Every sentence must make sense by itself and must contain a subject and a predicate. Fragments are pieces of sentences which do not make sense standing alone or do not contain a subject and a predicate.

*Examples:* Here are examples of common types of fragments and how they should be corrected:

| Sentence fragment (underlined part) | Corrected |
|---|---|
| I think he's guilty. <u>If you ask me.</u> | I think he's guilty, if you ask me. |
| I saw Bill. <u>Standing on the corner.</u> | I saw Bill standing on the corner. |
| We went with the Joneses. <u>Who live next door to us.</u> | We went with the Joneses, who live next door to us. |

*Correcting Your Error:* Correct your error by first finding the sentence fragment. Then join it either to the sentence ahead or the sentence that follows, wherever it seems to belong.
Write the corrected fragment here:

_____

*For Additional Practice:* To be sure you understand the error, try this corrective exercise. Some of the items below contain two complete sentences. Mark those *C* for correct. Some contain one sentence and a fragment. Correct those by rewriting the item to make it one complete sentence.

1. Wait for us. But do not wait more than fifteeen minutes.

2. Wait for us. Over there where the bus stops.

3. The Middle East has always been a land of conflict. Especially of a religious sort.

4. No matter how much we try to conserve. We will still need to import foreign oil.

5. Our own oil reserves are dwindling. And doing so at a very rapid rate.

Figure 21. Sample Corrective Exercise Form for Sentence Fragments.

# Bibliography

# Bibliography

Abrahamson, Richard F. *The Effects of Formal Grammar Instruction vs. the Effects of Sentence Combining Instruction on Student Writing: A Collection of Evaluative Abstracts of Pertinent Research Documents.* Houston: University of Houston, 1977.

Allen, R. R., and Brown, Kenneth C., eds. *Developing Communication Competence in Children.* Skokie, Ill.: National Textbook, 1976.

Allred, Ruel A. *Spelling: The Application of Research Findings.* Washington, D.C.: National Education Associates, 1977.

Applebee, Arthur N. "Teaching Conditions in Secondary School English: Highlights of a Survey." *English Journal* 67 (March 1978): 57–65.

Applebee, Arthur N. *Tradition and Reform in the Teaching of English: A History.* Urbana, Ill.: National Council of Teachers of English, 1974.

Bamberg, Betty. "Composition Instruction Does Make a Difference: A Comparison of the High School Preparation of College Freshmen in Regular and Remedial English Classes." *Research in the Teaching of English* 12 (1978): 47–59.

Beach, Richard, and Cooper, Charles. "Response to Literature." In *Perspectives on Research in English, Education, and Reading,* Michael F. Graves and Stephen M. Koziol, eds. Urbana, Ill.: National Council of Teachers of English, 1974.

Becker, Wesley C. "Teaching Reading and Language to the Disadvantaged— What We Have Learned from Field Research." *Harvard Educational Review* 47 (November 1977): 518–543.

Bledsoe, Eugene. "Teaching about Divorce." In *Thematic Units in Teaching English and the Humanities,* 1st suppl. Urbana, Ill.: National Council of Teachers of English, 1977.

Block, James H., and Anderson, Lorin W. *Mastery Learning in Classroom Instruction.* New York: Macmillan, 1975.

Block, James H., and Burns, Robert B. "Mastery Learning." In *Review of Research in Education* 4, Lee S. Shulman, ed. Itasca, Ill.: F. E. Peacock, 1977.

Bloom, Benjamin. *Alterable Variables: The New Direction in Educational Research.* Edinburgh: Lindsay, 1979.

Bloom, Benjamin. *Human Characteristics and School Learning: A Theory of School Learning.* New York: McGraw Hill, 1976.

Blount, Nathan. "Research on Teaching Literature, Language, and Composition." In *Second Handbook of Research on Teaching,* Robert M. Travers, ed. Chicago: Rand McNally, 1973.

Bobbitt, Franklin. *How to Make a Curriculum.* New York: Houghton Mifflin, 1924.

Boehnlein, Mary, and Ritty, James. "Integration of the Communication Arts Curriculum: A Review." *Language Arts* 54 (April 1977): 372-77.

Bordie, John G. "Language Tests and Linguistically Different Learners: The Sad State of the Art." In *Research Bases for Oral Language Instruction,* Thomas D. Horn, ed. Urbana, Ill.: National Conference on Research in English, 1971.

Brunetti, Gerald J. "The Bullock Report: Some Implications for American Teachers and Parents." *English Journal* 67 (November 1978): 58-64.

Bullock, Alan, chrm. *A Language for Life.* Report of the Committee of Inquiry Appointed by the Secretary of State for Education and Science. London: Her Majesty's Stationery Office, 1975.

Buros, Oscar K. *English Tests and Reviews.* Edison, N.J.: Gryphon Press, 1975.

College Entrance Examination Board, Commission on English. *Freedom and Discipline in English.* New York: College Entrance Examination Board, 1965.

Cooper, Charles R., and Petrosky, Anthony R. "A Psycholinguistic View of the Fluent Reading Process." *Journal of Reading* 19 (December 1976): 184-207.

Copperman, Paul. *The Literacy Hoax.* New York: William Morrow, 1978.

Cusick, Philip A. *Inside High School: The Student's World.* New York: Holt, 1973.

Devine, Thomas G. "Listening: What Do We Know after Fifty Years of Research and Theorization?" *Journal of Reading* 21 (January 1978): 296-304.

Dewey, Evelyn. *The Dalton Laboratory Plan.* New York: E. P. Dutton, 1922.

Diederich, Paul B. *Research 1960-70 on Methods and Materials in Reading.* Princeton, N. J.: ERIC Clearinghouse on Tests, Measurement, and Evaluation, 1973.

Di Vesta, Francis J., and Palermo, David S. "Language Development." In *Review of Research in Education* 2, Fred N. Kerlinger and John B. Carroll, eds. Itasca, Ill.: F. E. Peacock, 1974.

Dixon, John. *Growth Through English.* Reading G.B.: National Association for the Teaching of English, 1967.

Drost, David. "Error Analysis: Fewer Errors and Faster Grading." In *How to Handle the Paper Load,* Gene Stanford, ed. Urbana, Ill.: National Council of Teachers of English, 1979.

Early, Margaret J. "What Does Research in Reading Reveal about Successful Reading Programs?" In *What We Know about High School Reading: What Does Research in Reading Reveal?,* M. Agnella Gunn, ed. Urbana, Ill.: National Conference on Research in English, 1969.

Educational Policies Commission. *Education for All American Youth.* Washington, D.C.: National Education Association, 1944.

Eisner, Elliott W. *The Educated Imagination.* New York: Macmillan, 1979.

English, Fenwick W. *Quality Control in Curriculum Development.* Arlington, Va.: American Association of School Administrators, 1978.

Fraser, Ian S., and Hodson, Lynda M. "Twenty-One Kicks at the Grammar-House." *English Journal* 67 (December 1978): 49-54.

Geedy, Patricia S. "What Research Tells Us about Spelling." *Elementary English* 52 (February 1975): 233-35.

Goodlad, John I. "What Goes On in Our Schools." *Educational Researcher* 6 (1977): 3-6.

Graves, Michael F.; Palmer, Rebecca L.; and Furniss, David A. *Structuring Reading Activities for English Classes.* Urbana, Ill.: ERIC Clearinghouse on Reading and Communication Skills, 1976.

Gunn, M. Agnella, ed. *What We Know About High School Reading: What Does Research in Reading Reveal?* Urbana, Ill.: National Conference on Research in English, 1969.

Hatfield. W. Wilbur, chrm. *An Experience Curriculum in English: A Report of the Curriculum Commission of the National Council of Teachers of English.* New York: D. Appleton Century, 1935.

Havighurst, Robert J. *Developmental Tasks and Education.* Chicago: University of Chicago Press, 1948.

Haynes, Elizabeth. "Using Research in Preparing to Teach Writing." *English Journal* 67 (January 1978): 82-88.

Hillocks, George, Jr. *Alternatives in English: A Critical Appraisal of Elective Programs.* Urbana, Ill.: National Council of Teachers of English, 1972.

Horn, Thomas D. "Spelling." In *Encyclopedia of Educational Research*, 4th ed., Robert L. Ebel, ed. New York: Macmillan, 1969.

Jewett, Arno. *English Language Arts in American High Schools.* U.S. Office of Education Bulletin 1958, no. 13. Washington, D.C.: Government Printing Office, 1959.

Karlin, Robert. "What Does Research Reveal about Reading and the High School Student?" In *What We Know about High School Reading: What Does Research in Reading Reveal?*, M. Agnella Gunn, ed. Urbana, Ill.: National Conference on Research in English, 1969.

Kenney, Robert W., et al. *Basic Competencies: A Manual of Information and Guidelines for Teachers and Administrators.* Montpelier: Vermont Department of Education, 1977.

Kilpatrick, William Heard. "The Project Method." *Teachers College Record* 19 (September 1918): 319-35.

Lundsteen, Sara, ed. *Help for the Teacher of Written Composition.* Urbana, Ill.: National Conference on Research in English, 1976.

Mandel, Barrett J. *Three Language-Arts Curriculum Models: Pre-Kindergarten through College.* Urbana, Ill.: National Council of Teachers of English, 1980.

Marten, Milton. "Listening in Review." In *Classroom-Relevant Research in Language Arts*, Harold G. Schane and James Walden, eds. Washington, D.C.: Association for Supervision and Curriculum Development, 1978.

Medley, Donald M. "The Effectiveness of Teachers." In *Research on Teaching: Concepts, Findings, and Implications*, Penelope L. Peterson and Herbert J. Walbert, eds. Berkeley: McCutchan Publishing, 1979.

Miller, Barbara, ed. *Minimum Competency Testing.* St. Louis: Central Midwestern Regional Educational Laboratory, 1978.

Moffett, James, and Wagner, Betty Jane. *Student-Centered Language Arts and Reading, K-13: A Handbook for Teachers*, 2nd ed. Boston: Houghton Mifflin, 1976.

Morrison, Henry C. *The Practice of Teaching in the Secondary School.* Chicago: University of Chicago Press, 1926.

Mueller, Daniel J. "Mastery Learning: Partly Boon, Partly Boondoggle." *Teachers College Record* 78 (1976): 41-52.

Muller, Herbert J. *The Uses of English.* New York: Holt, Rinehart, and Winston, 1967.

National Council of Teachers of English, Commission on the English Curriculum. *The English Language Arts in the Secondary School.* New York: Appleton Century Crofts, 1956.

National Council of Teachers of English, Committee on National Interest. *The National Interest and the Teaching of English: A Report on the Status of the Profession.* Urbana, Ill.: National Council of Teachers of English, 1961.

New Mexico State Department of Education. *Curriculum Planning Guide for the New Mexico Basic Skills Plan.* Santa Fe, N.M., n.d.

Okey, J. R. *Development of Mastery Teaching Materials.* Final evaluation report, USOE G-74-2990. Bloomington: Indiana University, 1975.

Oliver, Albert I. *Maximizing Mini-Courses: A Practical Guide to a Curriculum Alternative.* New York: Teachers College Press, 1978.

Olson, James W. "The Nature of Literature Anthologies Used in the Teaching of High School English 1917-57." Ph.D. dissertation, University of Wisconsin, 1969.

Ortony, Andrew. "Language Isn't for People: On Applying Theoretical Linguistics to Practical Problems." *Review of Educational Research* 45 (Summer 1975): 485-504.

Page, William D., and Pinnell, Gay Su. *Teaching Reading Comprehension.* Urbana, Ill.: ERIC Clearinghouse on Reading and Communication Skills, 1979.

Petrosky, Anthony R. "Response to Literature." *English Journal* 66 (October 1977): 96-98.

Pipho, Chris. *State Activity: Minimal Competency Testing.* Denver: Education Commission of the States, 1978.

Polanyi, Michael. *The Tacit Dimension.* Garden City, N.Y.: Doubleday, 1966.

Posner, George J., and Strike, Kenneth A. "A Categorization Scheme for Principles of Sequencing Content." *Review of Educational Research* 46 (Fall 1976): 665-90.

Purves, Alan C., and Beach, Richard. *Literature and the Reader.* Urbana, Ill.: National Council of Teachers of English, 1972.

Rogers, Carl R. *Freedom to Learn.* Columbus, Ohio: Charles E. Merrill, 1969.

Rosenshine, Barak V. "Content, Time, and Direct Instruction." In *Research on Teaching: Concepts, Findings, and Implications*, Penelope L. Peterson, and Herbert J. Walberg, eds. Berkeley: McCutchan, 1979.

Sand, Ole. "Curriculum Change." In *The Curriculum: Retrospect and Prospect: The Seventieth Yearbook of the National Society for the Study of Education*, Robert M. McClure, ed. Chicago: University of Chicago Press, 1971.

"Schools Mainly a Baby-Sitting Service, Not Goal Oriented, Goodlad Observes." *ASCD News Exchange*, 21, 3 (April 1979). Washington, D.C.: Association for Supervision and Curriculum Development.

Schwab, Joseph J. "The Practical: A Language for Curriculum." *The School Review* 78 (November 1969): 1–23.

Sherwin, J. Stephen. *Four Problems in Teaching English: A Critique of Research*. Scranton, Pa.: International Textbooks, 1969.

Smith, Dora V. *Evaluating Instruction in Secondary School English: A Report of a Division of the New York Regents' Inquiry into the Character and Cost of Public Education in New York State*. Chicago: National Council of Teachers of English, 1941.

Smith, Dora V. *Instruction in English*. Bureau of Education Bulletin 1932, no. 17. National Survey of Secondary Education Monograph, no. 20. Washington, D.C.: Government Printing Office, 1933.

Spann, Sylvia, and Culp, Mary Beth, eds. *Thematic Units in Teaching English and the Humanities*, 1st suppl. Urbana, Ill.: National Council of Teachers of English, 1977.

Squire, James R. "What Does Research in Reading Reveal about Attitudes Toward Reading?" In *What We Know About High School Reading: What Does Research in Reading Reveal?*, M. Agnella Gunn, ed. Urbana, Ill.: National Conference on Research in English, 1969.

Squire, James R., and Applebee, Roger K. *High School English Instruction Today: The National Study of High School English Programs*. New York: Appleton Century Crofts, 1968.

Stotsky, Sandra L. "Sentence-Combining as a Curricular Activity: Its Effect on Written Language Development and Reading Comprehension." *Research in the Teaching of English* 9 (Spring 1975): 30–71.

Sutton, Gary A. "Do We Need to Teach a Grammar Terminology?" *English Journal* 65 (December 1976): 37–40.

Task Force on Measurement and Evaluation in the Study of English. *Common Sense and Testing in English*. Urbana, Ill.: National Council of Teachers of English, 1975.

Thompson, Richard. "Individualized Reading: A Summary of Research." *Educational Leadership* 33 (October 1975): 56–65.

Tyler, Ralph. *Basic Principles of Curriculum and Instruction*. Chicago: University of Chicago Press, 1950.

Van De Weghe, Richard. *Research in Written Composition: Fifteen Years of Investigation*. Las Cruces: New Mexico State University, 1978.

Walker, Decker F. "Toward Comprehension of Curricular Realities." In *Review of Research in Education*, L. S. Shulman, ed. Itasca, Ill.: F. E. Peacock, 1977.

Walker, Decker F., and Schaffarzick, Jon. "Comparing Curricula." *Review of Educational Research* 44 (Winter 1974): 83–112.

Weaver, Constance. *Grammar for Teachers: Perspectives and Definitions.* Urbana, Ill.: National Council of Teachers of English, 1979.

Weaver, Phyllis, and Shonkoff, Fred. *Research Within Reach: A Research-Guided Response to Concerns of Reading Educators.* St. Louis: Central Midwestern Regional Educational Laboratory, 1978.

Weeks, Ruth M., ed. *A Correlated Curriculum.* New York: D. Appleton Century Crofts, 1936.

Wolcott, Harry F. *Teachers Versus Technocrats: An Educational Innovation in Anthropological Perspective.* Eugene: Center for Educational Policy and Management (University of Oregon), 1977.

Wolvin, Andrew D., and Coakley, Carolyn G. *Listening Instruction.* Urbana, Ill.: ERIC Clearinghouse on Reading and Communication Skills, 1979.

Wright, Grace S. *Core Curriculum in Public High Schools: An Inquiry into Practices, 1949.* U.S. Office of Education, bull. 1950, no. 5. Washington, D.C.: Government Printing Office, 1950.

# Author

Allan A. Glatthorn is Associate Professor in education at the University of Pennsylvania. He holds degrees from Temple University, has been an Alfred North Whitehead Fellow at Harvard University, and a John Hay Fellow at the University of Chicago. He was director of the NCTE Commission on Curriculum, was a member of the National Council for the Humanities, and is a member of the National Humanities Faculty. He taught high school English and was a department head and principal of Abington High School before joining the faculty of the University of Pennsylvania. He is coauthor of several English textbooks and is the senior author of *Composition Skills*.